HAL LEONARD

AUTOHARP METHOD

BY RAY CHOI

To access video, visit:
www.halleonard.com/mylibrary
Enter Code
6253-2792-3604-1241

ISBN 978-1-4950-7124-9

HAL•LEONARD®
7777 W. BLUEMOUND RD. P.O. BOX 13819 MILWAUKEE, WI 53213

In Australia Contact:
Hal Leonard Australia Pty. Ltd.
4 Lentara Court
Cheltenham, Victoria, 3192 Australia
Email: ausadmin@halleonard.com.au

Visit Hal Leonard Online at
www.halleonard.com

CONTENTS

ABOUT THE AUTHOR

Ray Choi—a luthier in Tustin, CA—owns and operates Grace Music. Here, he has built over 650 custom autoharps with rich, resonating tones giving full volume through the warm and exotic woods he painstakingly selects. In addition, Ray has given lessons to over 600 students, serves as Music Director of his church, and gives public performances.

Although Ray plays woodwind instruments, mandolin, and guitar, he lives and breathes the autoharp. Over the years, he has developed a new technique dubbed the "hummingbird tremolo" because of its fast flutter of fingers across the strings. The hummingbird tremolo is similar to the sound of a mandolin and is a skill that took thousands of hours to perfect. In 2011, using this new technique, Ray Choi won first-place at both the Mount Laurel Autoharp Gathering and Walnut Valley International Music Festival, a feat only a few other autoharpists had ever accomplished.

The Oscar Schmidt Company (whose autoharps Ray has sold thousands over the years) calls him "Mr. Autoharp." Ray's passion for the autoharp resonates not only through his own handcrafted instruments, but also through his skill and dedication as a performer, educator, and essential part of the autoharp community. Ray truly lives and breathes the autoharp!

INTRODUCTION

Welcome to the *Hal Leonard Autoharp Method*. My passion for the autoharp and its exquisitely beautiful repertoire are the reasons I must share this instrument with you. Its potential is only now being discovered—it is no longer a simple parlor instrument or one you become acquainted with in kindergarten. It is more than just an instrument on which you can quickly learn to play a simple song or even strum along as it accompanies you while singing a melody. It is far more than that, and I am excited to take you on this exciting journey of discovery!

The autoharp has many virtues that make it an instrument of choice:

- It is one of the easiest instruments for beginners to learn.

- It is highly portable, weighing around 8–10 pounds.

- It can be used to play most genres of music.

- It can be played as a solo instrument or as accompaniment to others.

My goal in this book is to take you beyond basic strumming to beginning melody playing. In a carefully paced step-by-step process, you will learn enough music theory to read all basic music scores, which will enable you to play melodies and not just strum along with other musicians.

There are both right- and left-hand exercises throughout the book to prepare you for each song. My aim is to demystify all the autoharp tablature so you are thoroughly comfortable with your skills as you approach each new song.

Throughout this book, you will find photos and charts for further visual aid. In addition, you will find that the accompanying videos provide both audio and visual explanations for each song. You may wish to play along with me.

I sincerely hope your musical journey with the autoharp will be one of great success and much pleasure!

ABOUT THE VIDEO

 All of the accompanying videos for this book can be accessed online for streaming or download. Simply visit **www.halleonard.com/mylibrary** and enter the code found on page 1 of this book. Video examples are noted throughout the book with the icon seen here.

GETTING STARTED

THE EVOLUTION OF THE AUTOHARP

Mr. Charles F. Zimmerman, a proficient accordion player, had recently arrived in Philadelphia, PA, from Germany and had been repairing accordions when he invented the autoharp in 1881. His whole purpose for inventing the autoharp was not to offer the world a new instrument to play, but to promote his new tone-numbering system. His lifelong passion was to revolutionize and simplify how we read music, thereby making it accessible to more people.

From this humble beginning, the autoharp soon became a popular parlor instrument in the late 1800s. Manufacturing of the Zimmerman autoharp commenced in 1885 and continued through 1899. However, when records were introduced in the early 1900s and people began listening to these sonic wonders, the autoharps retreated to the closets. Although no autoharps were manufactured between 1900 and 1910, the instrument was played extensively in the Appalachian area and became known as the "mountain piano." Several companies manufactured them until 1932, at which time Oscar Schmidt International began to produce the instrument. In 1940, Maybelle Carter of the Carter Family showed the world how delightful music could sound on her autoharp, and the world took notice. Sales of Oscar Schmidt autoharps increased and, to date, Oscar Schmidt has produced more autoharps than any other manufacturer.

As more and more people pursued the pleasure of playing the autoharp, new strumming techniques were developed and autoharpists expanded into a variety of musical genres. Because of this renewed enthusiasm, luthiers began to improve upon its tone, design, and features. Today, beautiful custom autoharps are crafted from exotic woods for professional and demanding autoharpists all over the world.

ANATOMY OF AN AUTOHARP

Autoharps typically have almost three octaves: two full octaves in the middle and upper registers, supported in the bass section with fewer than 12 strings. Most will have 36 strings. The 21-chord chromatic autoharp is most common, 21 being the maximum number of chord bars that can fit on the autoharp. Occasionally, you may also see autoharps with anywhere from three to 15 chord bars. Check out the picture of an autoharp below, with all its parts labeled.

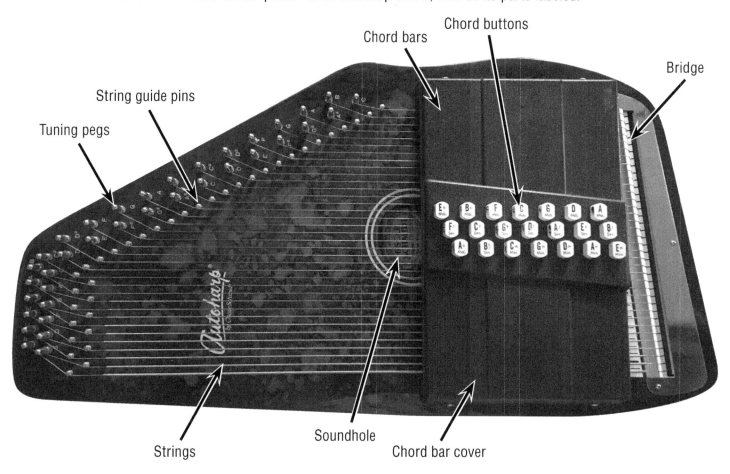

SELECTING AN AUTOHARP

There are two basic types of autoharps: *chromatic* and *diatonic*. A chromatic harp has up to seven major chords, along with supporting sevenths and minors. It has a string layout most similar to that of a piano, making it the most common choice for beginning autoharpists.

A diatonic autoharp has fewer major chords than a chromatic autoharp, and these majors are the chords that belong to a particular key—for example, the key of D. If it is a D diatonic autoharp, there may be only a total of three major chords: D, G, and A. The remaining chord bars can be used to create sevenths, minors, and colorful chords like Dmaj7 or Gsus4. These are beautiful chords, but the drawback is you are now limited to playing only in the key of D. To solve this issue and allow more options, you may eventually choose to have both a chromatic and at least one diatonic autoharp.

Once you have decided on either a chromatic or diatonic autoharp, you will want to consider your budget. Autoharps are available on internet auction sites, but be sure to purchase only from reputable sellers, as the condition of the instrument cannot always be determined from photos. You can also purchase an autoharp from an online store. You may wish to buy a manufactured autoharp, such as an Oscar Schmidt. However, if you desire custom wood and special features, you will need to purchase from a luthier. Luthiers will provide you with the chord-layout pattern of your choice, taking into consideration how many chord bars you want and whether you want chromatic or diatonic. They can also add a fine-tuning system or a pickup for amplification. In addition, a luthier will hand-carve your autoharp out of fine woods to produce the sound you most prefer. The types of wood (some of which are exotic), upgraded chord bars, strings, improved internal structure for added volume, fine tuning system, and other custom elements all add to the instrument's sound quality and durability.

TUNING YOUR AUTOHARP

It is essential to always keep your autoharp in tune. There are several reasons for this. First and foremost, it is courteous to others to play an instrument that is in tune. Also, the more you play an instrument that is in tune, the better recognition of correct pitch you will develop.

You may only need to tune once a week, or as often as three times a day. How often you need to tune depends on several factors:

- How often you play

- How hard you strum the strings

- Variations in humidity and temperature where you keep your autoharp

- The age of your autoharp

If you have a new autoharp or have recently restrung an older one, you will need to tune more frequently—loosening and tightening the strings until they become stabilized. Exposure to changes in humidity, as well as to heat and cold, greatly affect the tension of the strings. Be careful not to leave your autoharp in a hot car for any period of time or out in the sunlight on a hot day. When traveling, do not leave your autoharp in the trunk of your car but, rather, keep it with you in the vehicle where there is climate control. Extreme heat can cause an autoharp to implode upon itself. Keeping it in its case and away from sunlight is the best way to store an autoharp even in your home.

The tuning pins on the left side of the autoharp are tightened or loosened using a large wrench (see photo on the next page), which was most likely included with the purchase of your autoharp. Some autoharps have what is called a fine-tuning system on its right side. If you have this feature, you can do just what the name suggests: fine tune the strings. With the convenience of a fine-tuning system, you are able to tune the harp more accurately by making small turns with a special T-shaped wrench that has a handle across the top (see photo). The size of this wrench varies from manufacturer to luthier. In addition to wrenches, you will need a tuning device, such as the type used to tune a guitar. There are many electronic tuners available with prices starting at $15. If you have a pickup with a quarter-inch jack along the side of your autoharp, you can use an electronic tuner that can be simply plugged in (see photo). The electronic tuning device needs to be set at A440 pitch. This type of tuner offers better accuracy than one that does not plug in. In addition, it will enable you to tune the bass strings, which often do not register on other devices. The extra expense can ensure precision and save you much time when tuning.

The process of tuning varies depending on how out of tune your instrument is. If it is only slightly out of tune, you may start at the top or bottom of the strings and work your way to the other end. If it is greatly out of tune, it is advisable to select only one note at a time, tuning all the octaves of that note. Then move on to another note, tuning all its octaves, and so forth, until all of the strings have been tuned. In this fashion, you will not put any undue tension upon any section of the strings, which can create tension on the autoharp's frame. There is approximately 1,675 pounds of tension on the autoharp's strings.

| Large Tuning Wrench | T-Shaped Tuning Wrench | Electronic Tuner |

HOLDING YOUR AUTOHARP

It is essential for you to be comfortable when holding and playing your autoharp. In the early years, the autoharp was laid across a table or on a lap. In the 1940s, however, Maybelle Carter of the Carter Family demonstrated that you had more flexibility if you stood up and held it across your chest (see photo). Most folks use a strap that fastens to two metal pegs on the sides of the autoharp, so that you can easily stand while playing. "Slider" is a popular brand of strap, and it adjusts easily to your body height and girth. Another solution is simply a guitar strap.

If you prefer to sit when playing (see photo), you may need to place a beanbag or something similarly shaped on your lap to properly position the autoharp for playing.

When standing or sitting, the autoharp should be held at an angle, with the top about even with your left ear. Your left arm should not cross over the tuning pins—instead, they should cross over the opening between the pins and the chord bars as you reach for the chord bars. For left-handed players, simply reverse these directions.

Standing

Sitting

CHOOSING YOUR PICKS

There are many different types of picks for you to choose from. These include brass (which is a softer and more pliable metal), a firmer stainless steel, and plastic. Typically, plastic picks will have a softer sound on the strings, whereas metal will by nature sound metallic or harsh but will also produce a clear and loud tone. You will also find what is called a "speed pick," a plastic pick with a long, pliable protrusion at its end where it connects with the strings (see photo). The type of pick you choose may depend on the type of song you are playing. For example, a clear tone is necessary to play fast songs, and therefore metal picks work best. Slow songs, such as hymns and ballads, sound best when played with plastic picks.

While some people like a pick on every finger, most settle for three picks for their fingers plus a thumb pick (see photo). This is a matter of personal preference to suit your style of playing.

Whichever types of picks you select, the most important criterion is that they fit snugly on your thumb and fingers. If you find yourself with a pick that is loose, try wrapping medical or electrical tape around your finger after the pick is on. Position the pick so that up to a quarter inch hangs over your fingernail. This will help keep the pick stable so that it stays on your finger and does not slide off or to the side.

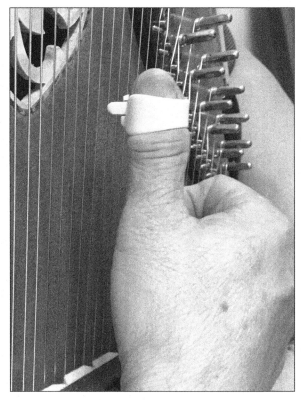

Speed Pick

Thumb and Finger Picks

FINGER INDICATIONS

For both your strumming hand and chord-bar hand, your thumb and fingers are indicated in written music the same way. Instead of 1-2-3-4-5, they are:

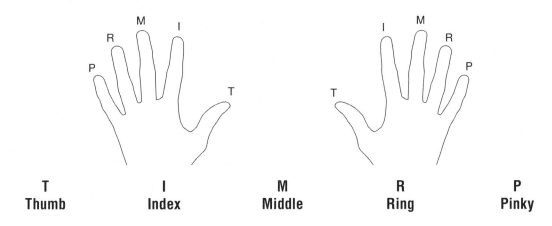

T	**I**	**M**	**R**	**P**
Thumb	**Index**	**Middle**	**Ring**	**Pinky**

BASIC MUSIC NOTATION

THE STAFF AND CLEF SIGNS

Song melodies are written with notes on a **staff**, which has five lines and four spaces in between.

At the beginning of each staff is a **clef sign**—either **bass clef** or **treble clef** (shown below). The type of clef used is dictated by the note range of the instrument you are playing. For autoharp, we use the treble clef.

Bass clef   **Treble clef**

To aid in the counting of the beats of a song, the notes are grouped in **measures** (or **bars**). Each measure has the same count, such as four beats per measure. The measures are identified and separated by **bar lines**. At the end of a song, you will see a **terminal bar line**. Sometimes **double bar lines** are used for the same purpose or to indicate the start of a new section.

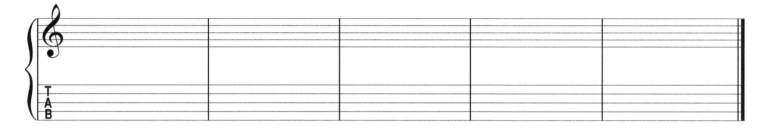

Note: The **tablature** staff (or **tab** staff) below the treble clef staff is where our autoharp tablature, showing strum patterns, will reside.

COMMON NOTE VALUES

Below are the most common types of notes and their **values**, or durations (how long they ring out for).

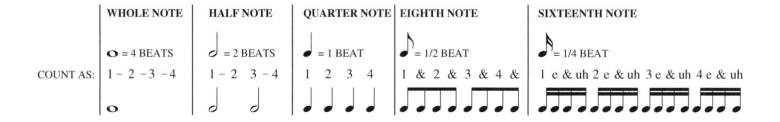

	WHOLE NOTE	HALF NOTE	QUARTER NOTE	EIGHTH NOTE	SIXTEENTH NOTE
	𝅝 = 4 BEATS	𝅗𝅥 = 2 BEATS	♩ = 1 BEAT	♪ = 1/2 BEAT	♬ = 1/4 BEAT
COUNT AS:	1 – 2 – 3 – 4	1 – 2 3 – 4	1 2 3 4	1 & 2 & 3 & 4 &	1 e & uh 2 e & uh 3 e & uh 4 e & uh

A **time signature** is displayed immediately after the clef sign and is made up of two numbers, one above the other. The top number indicates the number of beats per measure, and the bottom number indicates the value of each beat. In the example below, you will see what is called **four-four time** (or **4/4 time**). The top "4" means there are four beats per measure, and the bottom "4" tells us each quarter note receives one beat.

A time signature of **three-four time**, also called **three-quarter time** (or **3/4 time**), is displayed below. In 3/4 time, there are three beats per measure and the quarter note receives one beat.

NOTE NAMES

If you wish to read music, you will need to first memorize the names of the notes on the treble clef. The notes used on the spaces between the lines are F–A–C–E, and the notes on the lines are E–G–B–D–F. It helps to memorize the notes in the spaces by remembering that FACE rhymes with "space." For the line notes, remember the acronym for the sentence **E**very **G**ood **B**oy **D**oes **F**ine. See below for the locations of the notes on the staff.

Space notes

F   A   C   E

Line notes

E   G   B   D   F

BEGINNING STRUMMING PATTERNS

In this book, a dash between the counting numbers tells you to hold the chord throughout those counts. For example, a chord played for a whole note will be held for four counts, and a chord played for a half note will be held for two counts.

LONG THUMB STRUM

Our first strum technique is a **long thumb strum**.

Starting at the bass end of your strings, drag your thumb in a long, diagonal strum toward the treble (high-note) strings. Do this slowly over the count of four beats, for the length of each measure as indicated in the tab staff. Using the middle finger of your chord hand, firmly press the C chord button while slowly dragging your strumming-hand thumb across the strings in a long, diagonal strum. (Note: In the example below, the "T" beneath the autoharp tab tells you to use your thumb for this exercise. Also, the symbol ⦚ indicates the long, diagonal strum.)

Now, looking at the string names on your harp, locate the middle C, E, G, and the next C string. These strings correspond to the notes written in the treble clef of the exercise below. The melody notes are there so you can hum along as you strum the autoharp. Later, you will learn to play the melody notes by actually plucking these exact strings. However, for now, the notes are present to accustom you to recognizing melody notes and so you can enjoy humming along. The **chord symbols** (in this instance "C") displayed immediately above the tab staff indicate which chord bar (or chord button) is to be depressed.

 Exercise 1

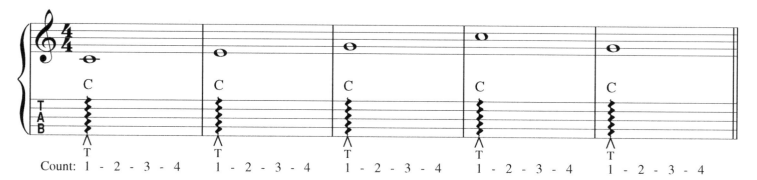

"Are You Sleeping?" is our first song, and it is written in the key of G. You will be pressing down firmly on the G chord button as you slowly strum long thumb strums, each held for four beats.

ARE YOU SLEEPING? (FRÈRE JACQUES)

morn-ing bells are ring-ing, morn-ing bells are ring-ing, ding, ding, dong, ding, ding, dong.

Below is a staff with three measures, the first and last one showing a **repeat sign**. When you reach the last repeat, it is time to skip back to the previous repeat bar and play those measures again.

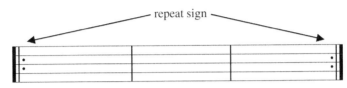

A **tie** simply means that you continue to hold (tie over) a note for the duration of itself plus the note to which it is tied. If a whole note is tied to another whole note, it lasts for the combined value of the two notes, or eight beats. Only the first tied note is picked.

Tied notes are shown as below:

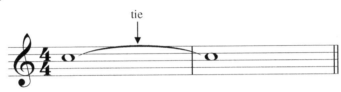

SHORT THUMB STRUM

Using only your strumming-hand thumb, make a short upward thumb strum (shown as ⋀) starting from the lower bass, then a second short upward thumb strum starting from the middle strings, followed by a third short upward thumb strum from the treble strings to the highest strings. This is the technique you will be using in Exercise 2 below. Because the example is in 3/4 time (waltz rhythm), be sure to emphasize the first of the three strums, making it louder than the second and third strums and, therefore, more pronounced.

The middle finger of the chord-button hand should be placed on the chord that has the same name as the key of the song. This position is called "home base" because this chord usually begins and ends the song. You will return frequently to this chord throughout the tune, as well. Use your index finger to play the A7 as this is a comfortable and natural position. Now, let's try the exercise.

 Exercise 2

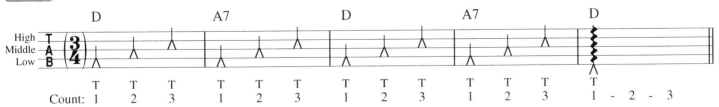

Our next song is written in 3/4 time and is played with two chords, D and A7. Throughout this piece, you'll see **dotted half notes** (♩.), which last for three beats each. When a **dot** follows a note, the value is increased by one half of the note's value. For instance: A half note equals two beats; half of two is one; two plus one is three—so, a dotted half note lasts for three beats.

Note the ties in measures 5 and 6 and in the last two measures. Also, notice the repeat sign at the end, which tells you to return to the previous repeat bar (at the beginning, in this case) to play and sing the second verse. On the accompanying video, the song is played only one time through.

 **DOWN IN THE VALLEY**

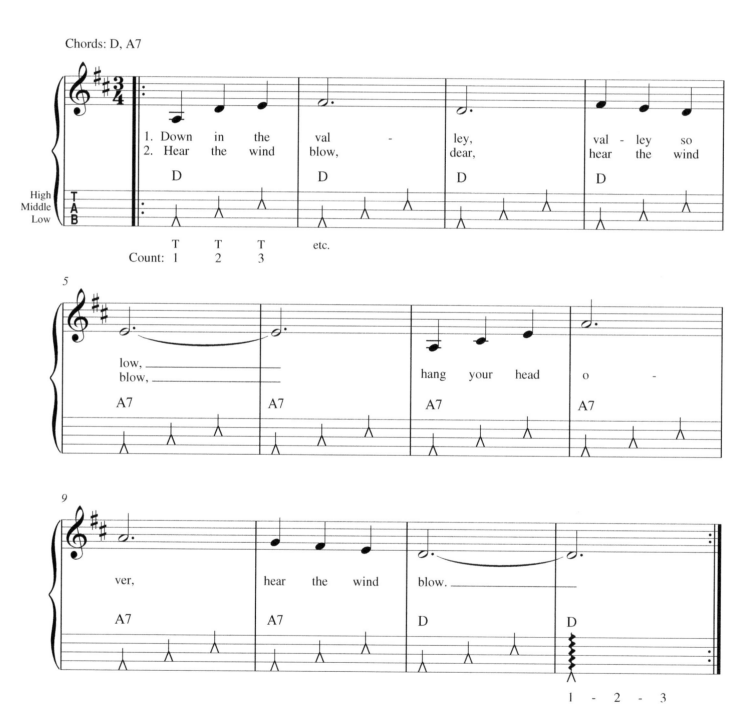

TWO-BEAT LONG THUMB STRUM

Using your long thumb strum and the chords C, G7, and F, you can now play "Jolly Old St. Nicholas." Here, each strum will be held for two beats. Consecutive vertical strum marks in the tab staff tell you to repeat the chord strum. Also remember, a dash between counting numbers indicates the strum is to be held for two beats (1–2 or 3–4).

Near the end of the song, there is a measure with a repeat sign, and above it, a bracket and number "1." This is a **first ending**, and it tells you to go back to the previous repeat bar. When you get to the first ending again, skip over it and play the next bracketed measure, the **second ending**, which has a number "2" above it. This enables you to end the song with a C chord (the home base) rather than a G7.

JOLLY OLD ST. NICHOLAS

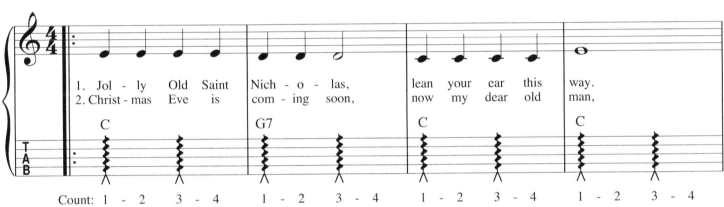

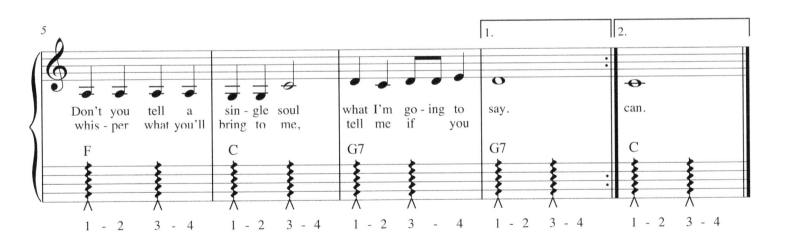

DOUBLE STRUM

To add some interest to our strumming pattern, we are going to learn a **double strum**. You will use your index finger, designated by an "I" below the tab staff. Covering only about four strings, it will be a shorter stroke than the long thumb stroke, which covers 9–12 strings. Your index finger will execute a light downward brush stroke, shown as ↓. So with your right thumb, strum an upward stroke and follow it immediately with a lighter, shorter downward brush strum with your index finger. Together, these two strums are a double strum.

 Exercise 3

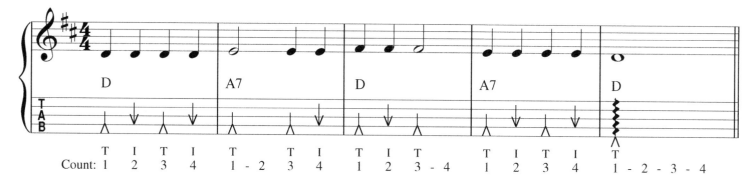

Notice below that the song "Aunt Rhody" has only one note in its first measure—this is a **pickup note**. If fewer than the expected number of beats appear in the first measure, it is called a **pickup measure**.

GO TELL AUNT RHODY

Chords: D, A7

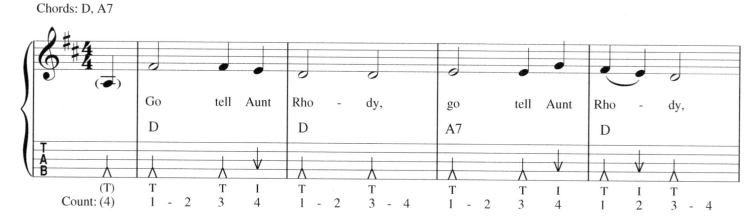

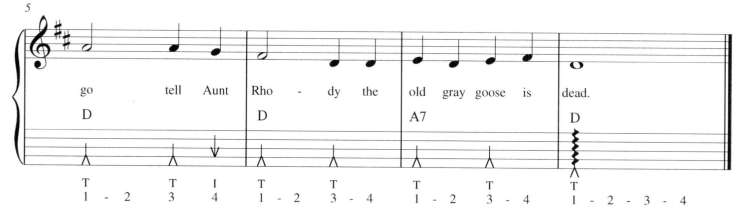

ALTERNATING THUMB STRUM

As we prepare to play "Michael, Row the Boat Ashore," note the two-beat pickup on a 4/4 time signature (start counting "one, two" and then come in on "three, four"). This three-chord song (D, G, and A7) will be played with a slightly different strumming pattern. The feel of this tune lends itself to a rocking motion, with the thumb simply strumming first in the bass and then the high strings, alternating back and forth. In the third measure, the strum is first low and is followed by three high strums as the voice carries the syllable for four counts. (Note: when there is a pickup, we start counting measure numbers at the first *full* measure.)

"Michael, Row the Boat Ashore" includes whole notes, half notes, quarter notes, eighth notes, and a dotted quarter note in the melody of the first and fifth measures. The dotted quarter note receives its single count plus one half more. The melody in these measures would be counted as "one, two and, three and, four."

Prior to playing "Michael, Row the Boat Ashore," practice Exercise 4. Watch for the strumming variation in the third measure.

 Exercise 4

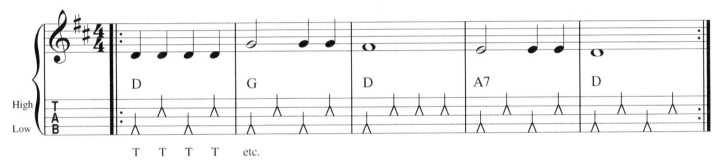

Now that you're comfortable with the strum pattern and chords, try "Michael, Row the Boat Ashore."

 MICHAEL, ROW THE BOAT ASHORE

Chords: D, G, A7

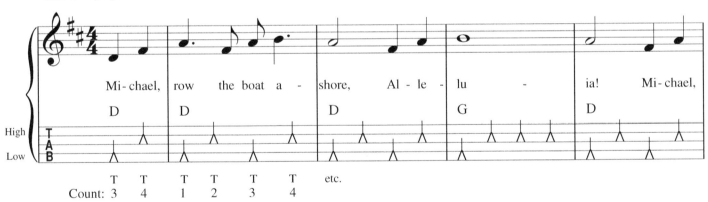

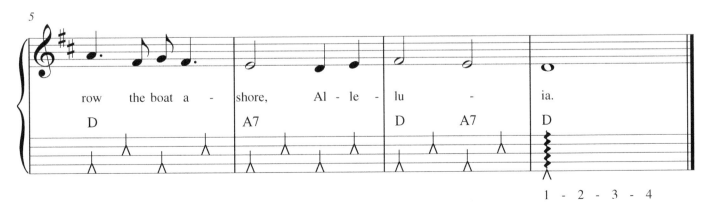

When brackets are shown in the tab (⌐), they illustrate what strum motions are to be played within a minimum of one beat. In the first measure of Exercise 5, the first long thumb strum is contained within a bracket. Under the bracket are the numbers 1–2, which mean to hold the strum for a duration of two beats. Likewise, 1–2–3–4 tells you to hold the strum for a duration of four beats. There can be more than one strum motion within one beat, as shown in measure 3 of this exercise; occurring within the second beat, a short upward thumb strum is followed by a short downward back brush with the index finger. These are eighth notes. Remember that an eighth note receives only half a beat.

 **Exercise 5**

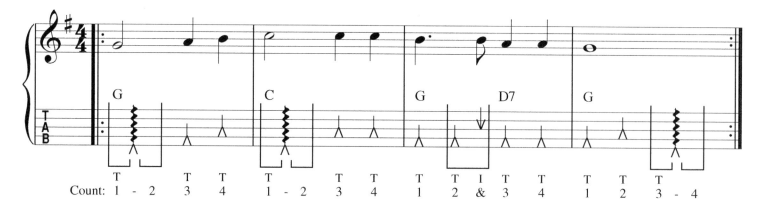

PUTTING THE PATTERNS TOGETHER

"Nearer, My God, to Thee," written in 4/4 time, utilizes all the strumming patterns you have learned so far. Varying your strumming patterns at the right time increases the musicality of your songs. Notice how the long upward thumb strum is held for two beats (measures 1, 2, etc.) and four beats (measures 4 and 8). Also, notice the alternating string sections (see measures 3, 5, 7, etc.).

Throughout this song, you will be strumming with your thumb, except for several places where you will follow a short upward thumb strum with a shorter back brush of the index finger. Together, these two movements take up one beat.

 **NEARER, MY GOD, TO THEE**

Chords: G, C, D7

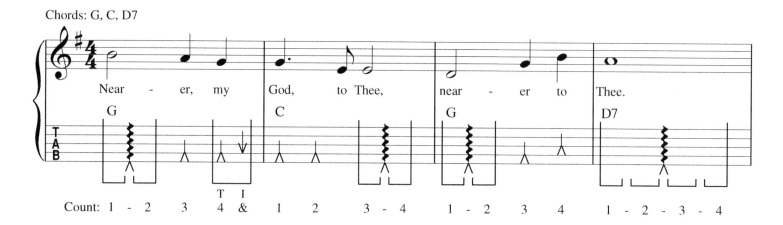

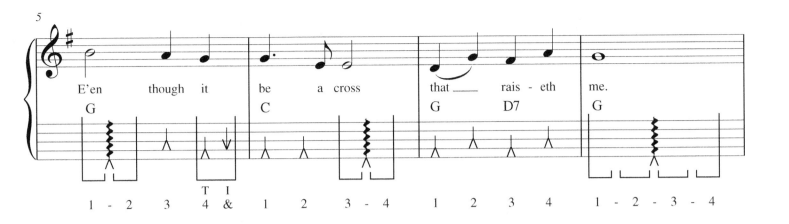

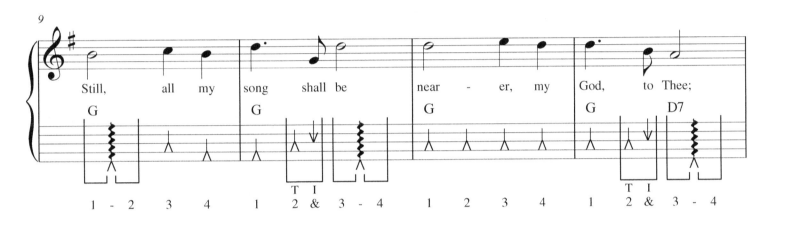

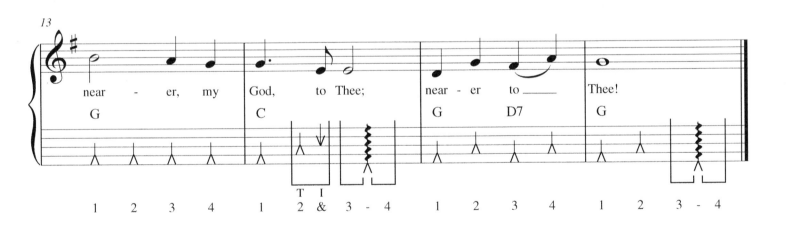

In "Amazing Grace (No. 1)," there are two music symbols that may be new to you. The first, *rit.*, stands for **ritardando**, which tells you to slow down rather than stay with the strict tempo of the song. You will usually encounter this at the end of a song.

The other music symbol is a **fermata**, shown as 𝄐. A fermata tells you to hold a note or chord longer than the strict beat would allow. Fermatas are usually used at the end of a song as well.

What really makes the following tune enjoyable to play and hear is the **modulation**, or key change, in the second verse. Here, a G7 transition chord is used to switch us to the key of C.

AMAZING GRACE (NO. 1)

Chords: G, D7, C, G7, F
Keys: G → C

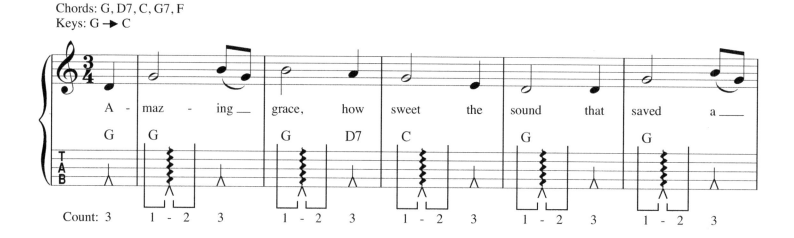

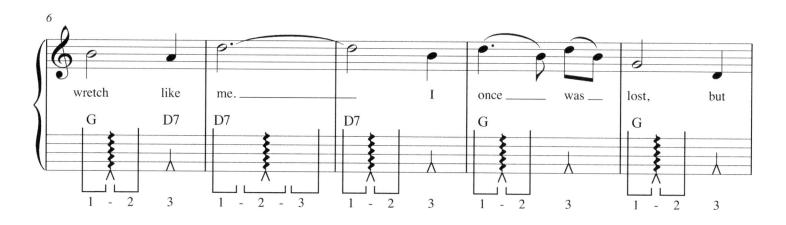

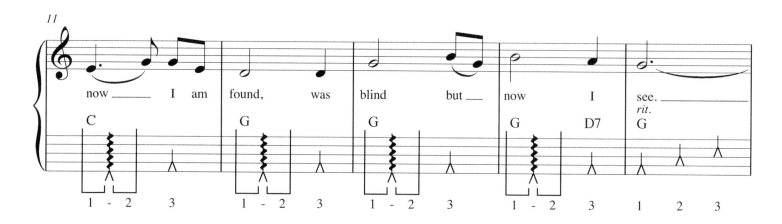

Modulation to Key of C

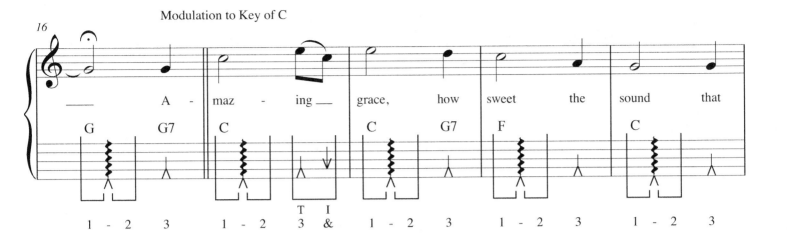

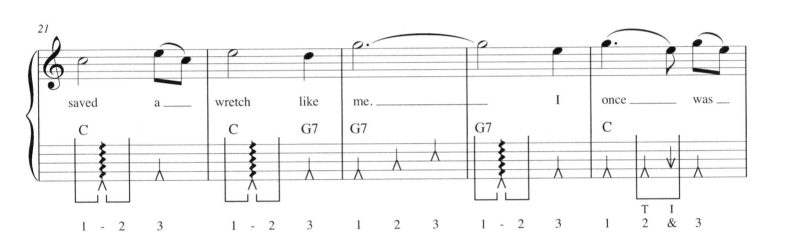

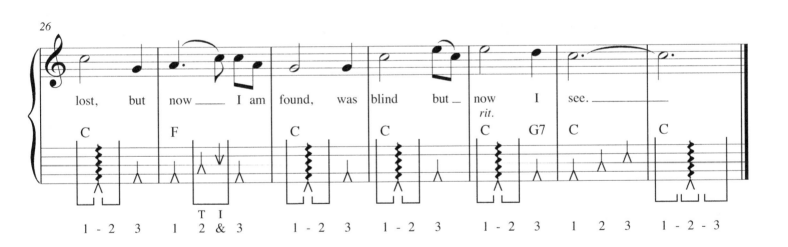

CHORD-HAND POSITION

Although there are different techniques for placing and then moving the fingers of the chord hand over the chord bar, I prefer one that is most efficient, thereby allowing me to play fast songs more easily. To minimize finger movement, I recommend the following placement of thumb and fingers, assuming your autoharp is an Oscar Schmidt.

Rest the middle finger on the chord-bar button that represents the key in which the song is written. It will share that button with the thumb and index finger immediately in front of it, giving it extra support and volume (see photo). This is the **I chord** ("one" chord), also called the **tonic chord** or **root chord**. In this case, the song is written in the key of A, so you would press your middle finger on the A chord button (or A7, as seen in the photo).

Your ring finger will play the chord immediately above (for example, the E7 chord, as seen in the photo). It will also be supported by the middle finger. This is the **V chord** ("five" chord), or **dominant chord**. It is called the "V chord" because its root is five notes above the root of the I chord. For example: A(1)–B(2)–C(3)–D(4)–E(5). E is the fifth note above A.

Your thumb will then play D7, the chord immediately below the A7 (as seen in the photo). Your index finger will support the thumb. This is the **IV chord** ("four" chord), or **subdominant chord**. It is called the "IV chord" because its root is four notes above the root of the I chord. For example: A(1)–B(2)–C(3)–D(4). D is the fourth note above A.

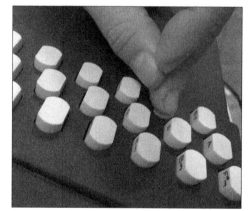 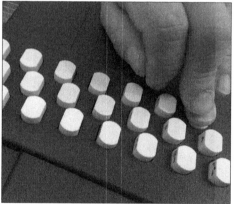 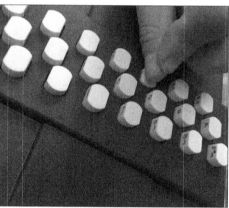

| I Chord Position | V Chord Position | IV Chord Position |

Take a moment now and place your middle finger on the C chord. Let's assume this is the key in which your song is written. What would then be the IV and V chords relative to this I chord? You will see that these three chords are laid out on your autoharp so that they are adjacent to each other, making it very easy to play your songs. (The IV chord is F and the V chord is G.)

Now, experiment a bit and place your finger on the F chord and assume it is the I chord. Strum the strings as you then change to the B♭ and C chords, the IV and V relative to F. Continue this exercise, playing each of the major chords along with their relative IV and V chords. Do you see how easily one can play a simple song written in one key and transpose it to another key? We'll talk more about this later.

Now that you have learned this placement of fingers and thumb over the chord-bar buttons, I am going to share with you my secret for moving to buttons that are farther away. When moving to any chord that is a long reach from your tonic (I chord), simply and quickly slide your thumb over that I chord where it will function as a placeholder—an anchor, so to speak. Now, you can reach to that distant chord and know with confidence you can accurately return to the I chord as soon as needed. This process brings you right back to home base.

Using this fingering method will not only increase efficiency so you may play fast when desired, but it will also enable you to play with more accuracy and volume.

The following chart shows the I, IV, V, and V7 chords for seven major keys. The fingers used to play the chords are shown as well.

Chord-Hand Reference Chart
(for 21-Chord Autoharp)

Tonic (I)	Subdominant (IV)	Dominant (V)	Dominant (V7)
M + TI	T + I	R + M	I
C	F	G	G7
D	G	A	A7
F	B♭	C	C7
G	C	D	D7
A	D	E	E7
B♭	E♭	F	F7
E♭	A♭	B♭	B♭7

CHORD-HAND PRACTICE NO. 1

Let's apply the concept we've been discussing to some exercises.

In the following examples, press the I, IV, V, and V7 chord buttons with your chord hand, while doing a short thumb strum with your strumming hand. Notice a box is placed around the I chord at the beginning and end of each line. Play the I chord with the middle finger along with the thumb and index finger. Then, play the IV chord with the thumb and index finger and return to the I chord. In the fourth measure, play the V chord with the ring finger along with the middle finger. In the seventh measure, you may play the G7 with the index finger alone, assuming you are playing an Oscar Schmidt autoharp. (Other autoharps may have a different chord layout, in which case, you'll need to experiment and decide which finger reaches the dominant seventh chord most easily.)

Each of the following lines offers two examples to practice: the top staff is in 4/4 time and the bottom is in 3/4. The slashes in each measure represent the chord strums. Additionally, each set of staves is in a different key: C, D, A, G, and F. Practice each key until you are comfortable with the chord-hand finger positions.

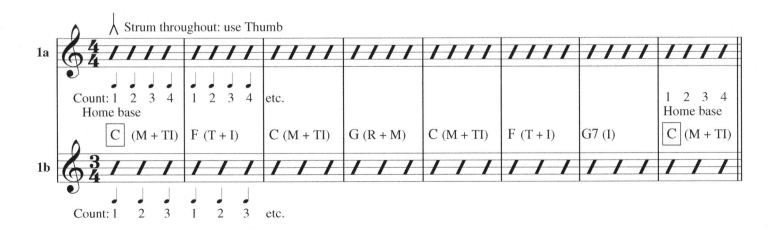

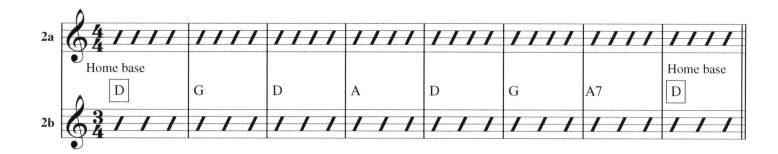

CHORD-HAND PRACTICE NO. 2

Now that you understand the positioning of the chord hand over the chord-bar buttons, we are going to practice anchoring the thumb on the key in which you are playing, which I like to call "home base." In our practice example, I have placed a box around that chord-bar button for emphasis. Because it is the tonic or root chord, you need to place your middle finger on it, also pressing down on it with the thumb and index finger.

Under the staff, you will see a triangle with a "T" inside it; this represents the anchor and tells you to hold down the root of the chord with the thumb, as the middle finger moves quickly to the minor or seventh chords (as shown in the subsequent measures). In Example 1, the third measure is played by the thumb and index finger, the fourth measure by the thumb and middle finger, the fifth measure by the thumb and index finger, and so forth—ending back on the home-base (tonic) chord.

Practice the five examples until you feel comfortable substituting the thumb as an anchor while quickly moving the middle finger to the next minor or seventh chord.

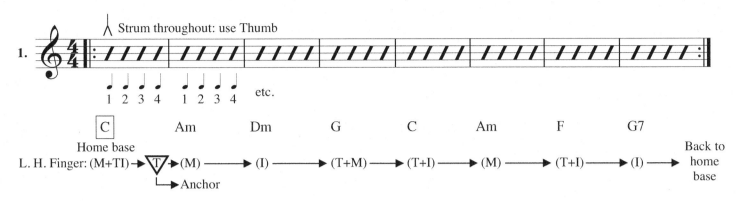

1. Strum throughout: use Thumb

1 2 3 4 1 2 3 4 etc.

| C | Am | Dm | G | C | Am | F | G7 |

Home base

L. H. Finger: (M+TI) → T → (M) → (I) → (T+M) → (T+I) → (M) → (T+I) → (I) → Back to home base

└→ Anchor

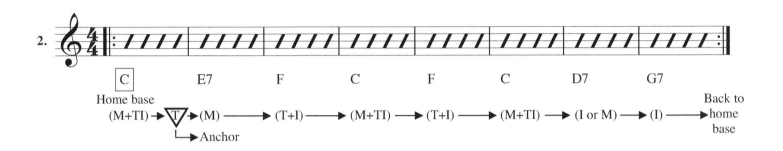

2.

| C | E7 | F | C | F | C | D7 | G7 |

Home base

(M+TI) → T → (M) → (T+I) → (M+TI) → (T+I) → (M+TI) → (I or M) → (I) → Back to home base

└→ Anchor

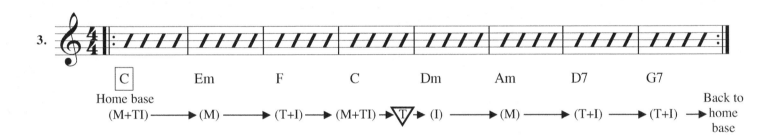

3.

| C | Em | F | C | Dm | Am | D7 | G7 |

Home base

(M+TI) → (M) → (T+I) → (M+TI) → T → (I) → (M) → (T+I) → (T+I) → Back to home base

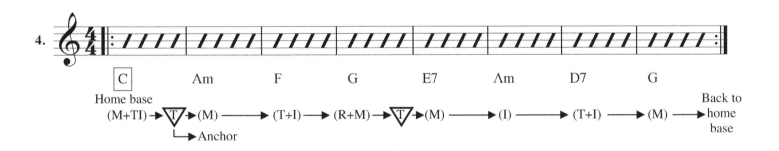

4.

| C | Am | F | G | E7 | Am | D7 | G |

Home base

(M+TI) → T → (M) → (T+I) → (R+M) → T → (M) → (I) → (T+I) → (M) → Back to home base

└→ Anchor

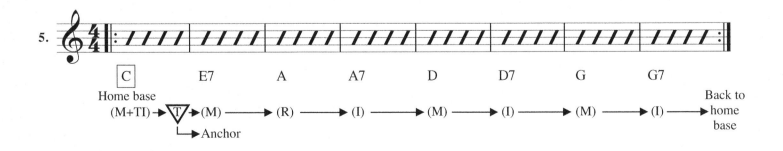

5.

| C | E7 | A | A7 | D | D7 | G | G7 |

Home base

(M+TI) → T → (M) → (R) → (I) → (M) → (I) → (M) → (I) → Back to home base

└→ Anchor

CHORD-HAND PRACTICE NO. 3

Now we are going to continue practicing the same anchor technique while using the F and G chords as tonics. Again, use the recommended fingering on the chord-bar buttons to easily and efficiently expedite the movement to the next minor or seventh chord.

In these examples, the strumming hand is playing four short thumb strums in each measure. Try counting out loud "one, two, three, four" as you strum the four beats, while focusing on moving your chord hand to the recommended chord-bar buttons.

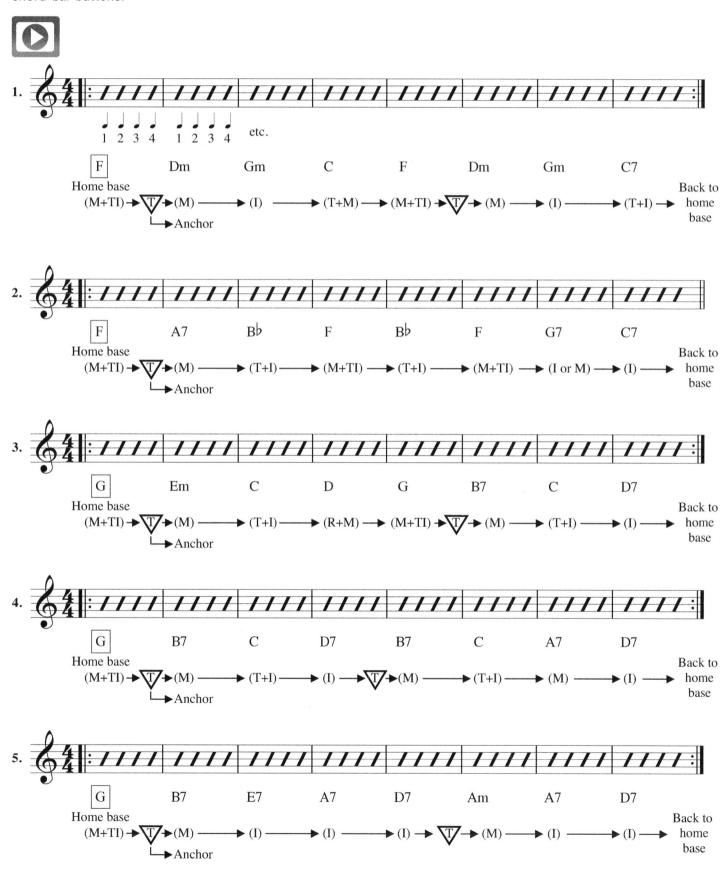

CHORD-STRUMMING SONGS

In this section, we'll apply what we've learned so far to some songs.

"Kumbaya," another popular song, is written in 3/2 time. This means there are three beats in each measure and the half note gets one beat. Therefore, the quarter note will receive only one half beat.

The strumming pattern mostly consists of alternating thumb strums and back brushes. The thumb strum is longer, followed by a shorter back brush with the index finger, designated as TI.

The other pattern is simply a lower thumb strum followed by a higher thumb strum.

You'll see a different type of counting pattern below the strums. This is used to accommodate the strums played here over the odd meter, in which each beat is divided into four equal parts ("one-e-and-uh, two-e-and-uh," etc.), instead of two ("one and, two and," etc.). You'll learn more about this type of counting pattern later in this section.

▶ KUMBAYA

Chords: C, F, G7

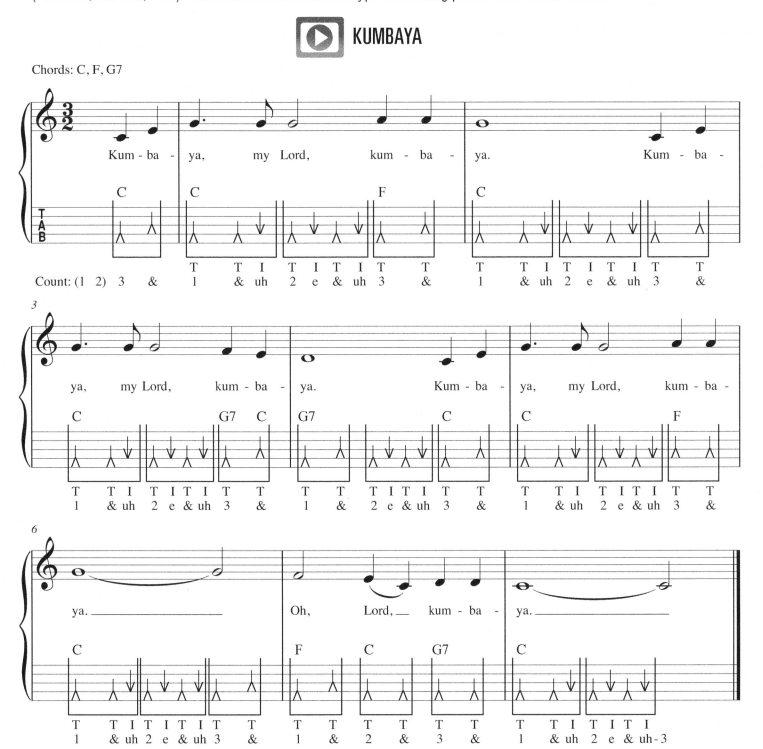

"Old Joe Clark (No. 1)" is a song that acquaints you with the location of three of your major-chord bars: G, C, and F.

A simple thumb strum is the only technique needed to play this song. (Remember, the "T" below the staff tells you to strum with the thumb.)

Notice the repeat signs at the end of the second and fourth lines, both in the tab and treble-clef staves. This song has an A and a B part—the first two lines are the A part, followed by the last two lines which are the B part.

The easiest finger placement on the chord bars is your middle finger on G, your index finger on C, and your thumb on F. By hovering your fingers just above the chord bars, you will be able to quickly and accurately locate them as you play along.

 OLD JOE CLARK (NO. 1)

Chords: G, C, F

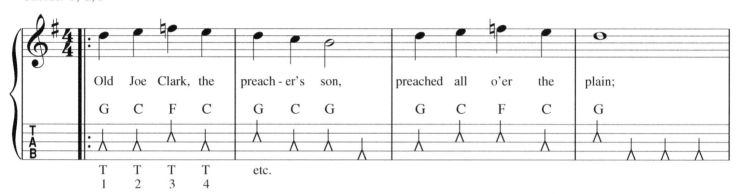

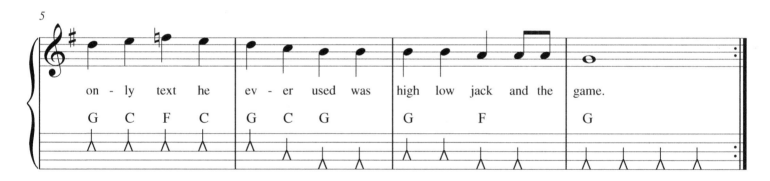

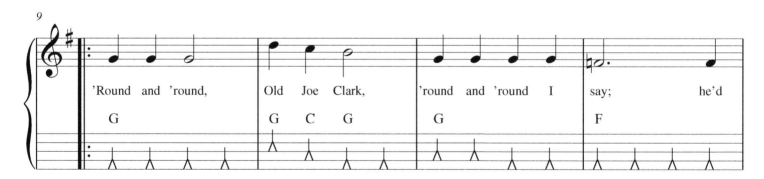

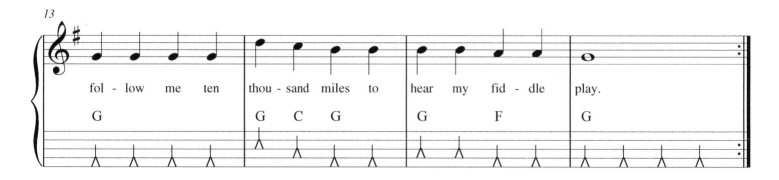

"This Old Man" is written in 2/4 time, so there are two beats in each measure and the quarter note receives one beat. It follows then that an eighth note will get half a beat, and a sixteenth note a quarter beat. It is easiest to count the measures in this song as "one and, two and."

The thumb will strum short strums alternately low and high across the autoharp, one strum for each half beat. There is a long thumb strum at the end, which is held for one full beat.

This short song is often sung as a round, so you would repeat it several times.

THIS OLD MAN

Chords: F, B♭, C7

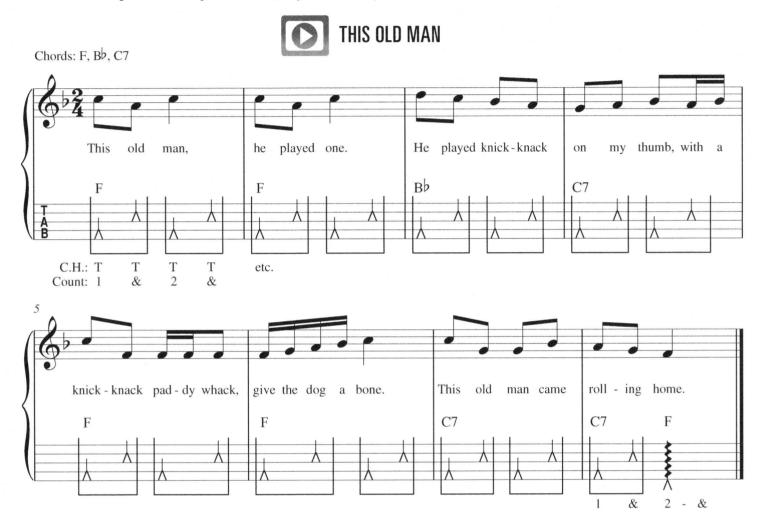

As we review the next song, "Clementine," you will notice a lot of dotted eighth notes followed by a sixteenth note. Together, those two notes take up the space of one quarter note. Sixteenth notes are counted "one-e-and-uh, two-e-and-uh, three-e-and-uh," etc. (This was the same type of counting pattern you used in the song "Kumbaya.") The dotted eighth note coincides with the first part of the beat ("one"), and the sixteenth note falls on the "uh" part of the beat. So the count for a dotted eighth and sixteenth combination is "1-uh, 2-uh," etc.

The song begins with a pickup on the third beat ("three-uh"). Each time you see a dotted eighth note followed by a sixteenth, strum upward with your thumb and then downward with a light brush stroke of your index finger.

Before you play the song, check out the following figure.

Chords: G, D7

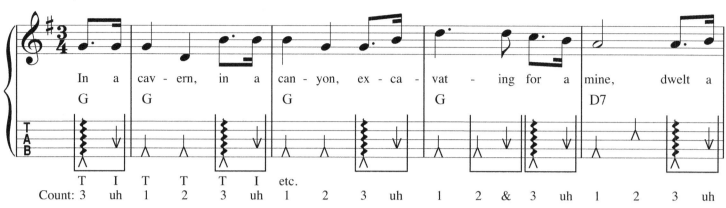

In a cav – ern, in a can – yon, ex – ca – vat – ing for a mine, dwelt a

Count: 3 uh 1 2 3 uh 1 2 3 uh 1 2 & 3 uh 1 2 3 uh

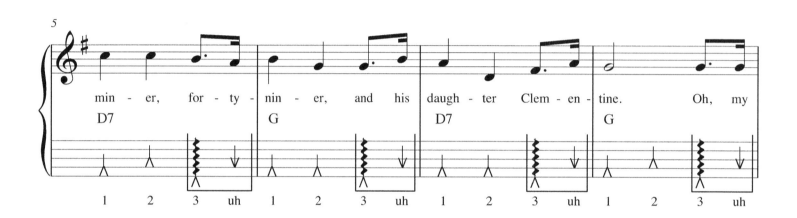

min – er, for – ty – nin – er, and his daugh – ter Clem – en – tine. Oh, my

1 2 3 uh 1 2 3 uh 1 2 3 uh 1 2 3 uh

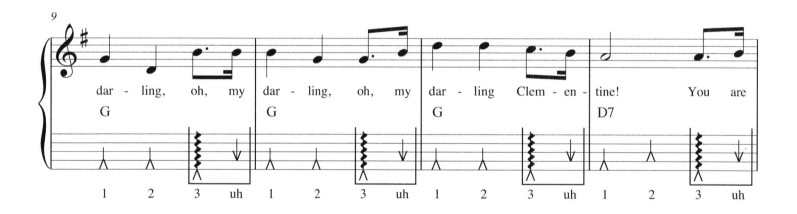

dar – ling, oh, my dar – ling, oh, my dar – ling Clem – en – tine! You are

1 2 3 uh 1 2 3 uh 1 2 3 uh 1 2 3 uh

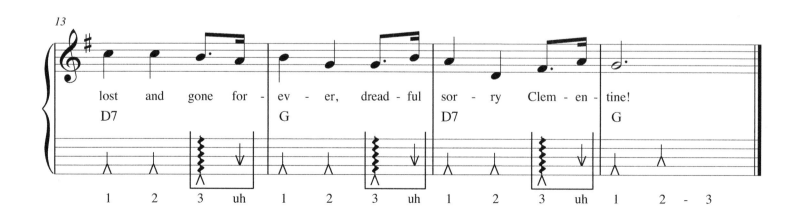

lost and gone for – ev – er, dread – ful sor – ry Clem – en – tine!

1 2 3 uh 1 2 3 uh 1 2 3 uh 1 2 – 3

"This Train" is written in **cut time**, signified by a "C" with a line through the middle: . Cut time is actually 2/2 time, which means there are two beats per measure and each half note receives one beat. Therefore, a quarter note will receive only one half beat.

Because this song uses a lot of "TI" (thumb strum followed by index back brush) along with single, short thumb strums, you will get good practice with this rhythm. Take the time to study the strum patterns until you are confident, and then try to sing the melody along with your strumming. This song offers good practice in singing against a rhythm with more strums than melody notes.

THIS TRAIN

Chords: D, A7, G

Let's look at two more songs with similar strums. The first tune includes **rests** in the vocal melody. Rests indicate a period of silence in music. Much like notes, rests have specific durations based on the symbol used:

WHOLE REST	HALF REST	QUARTER REST	EIGHTH REST	SIXTEENTH REST
= 4 BEATS	= 2 BEATS	= 1 BEAT	= 1/2 BEAT	= 1/4 BEAT

 CARELESS LOVE

Chords: F, C7, Bb

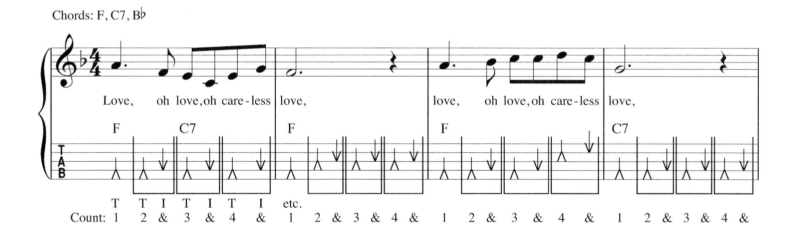

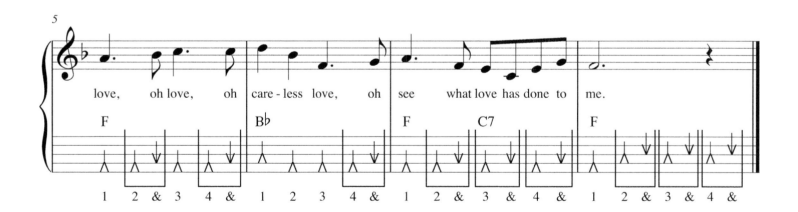

OLD TIME RELIGION

Chords: G, D7, C

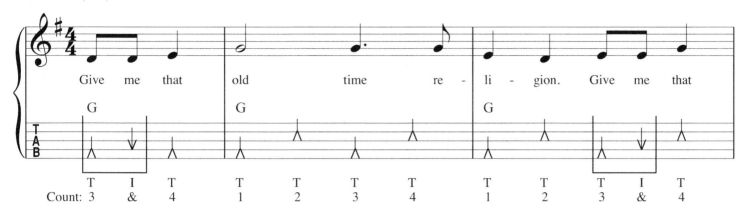

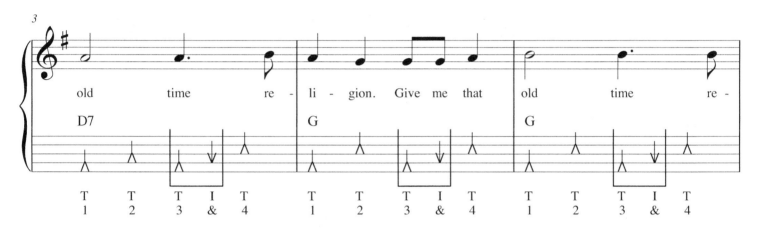

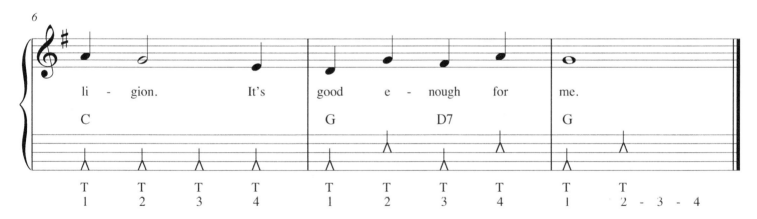

The next song, "Old Folks at Home" by Stephen Foster, has **syncopation** in the melody, which means the upbeats (the "ands") are emphasized rather than the downbeats (the numbers: 1, 2, 3, etc.). Your voice will carry the syncopated melody while your strumming hand keeps a steady 4/4 beat. You can most easily accomplish this by refraining from singing at first; concentrate on playing the music, which consists of simple one-beat thumb strums and the combination of the upward thumb strum followed by the downward index-finger brush stroke. Count out loud as you play. For example, the first measure is counted "one two-and three-and four-and." Once you are comfortable with the chords and rhythm, begin singing the syncopated melody along with your strumming. You will see that this song is a great exercise for using the thumb and index finger combination within one beat.

Chords: D, A, G, A7

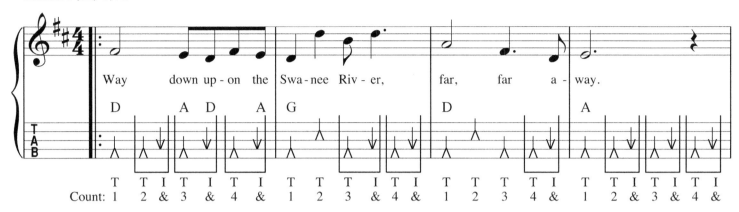

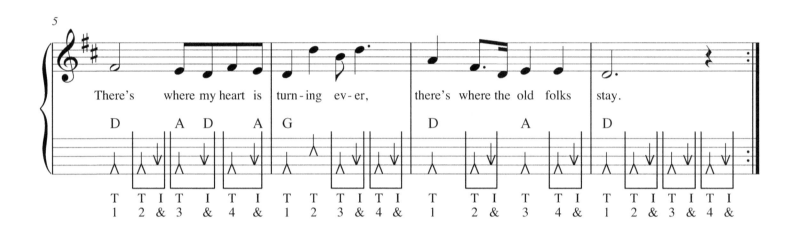

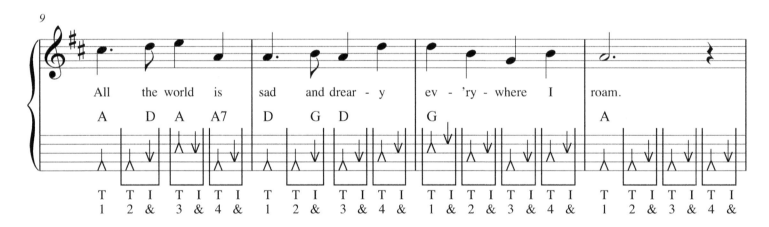

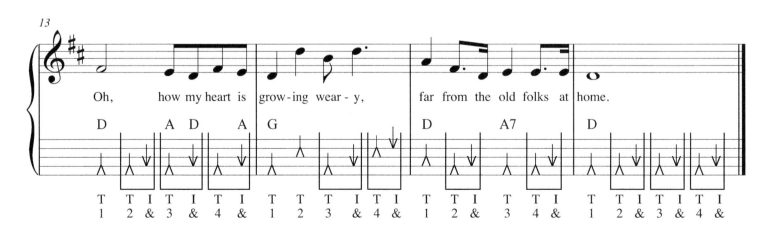

Let's try another tune with similar strumming.

 WHEN THE SAINTS GO MARCHING IN

Chords: G, D7, C

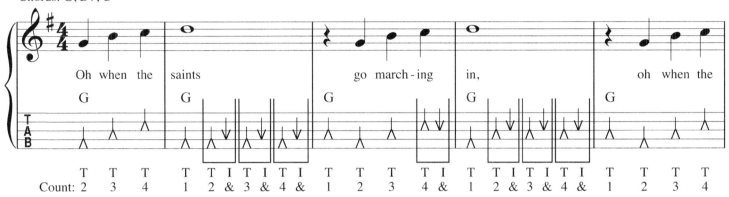

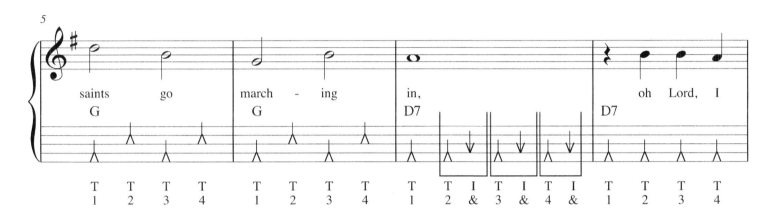

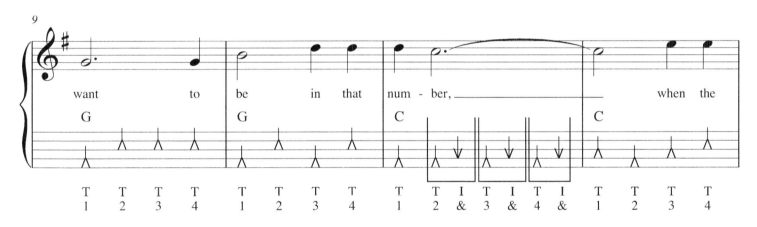

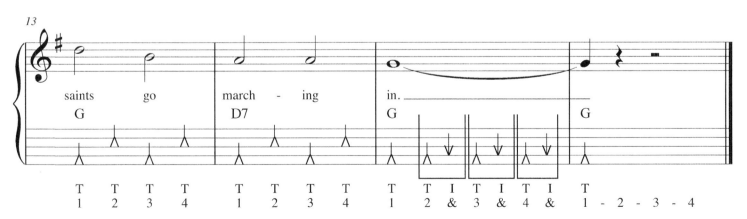

37

"Weggi's Song" is a little four-chord Swiss song that includes yodeling in its chorus. I suggest you become very familiar with the melody and strum pattern prior to adding the yodeling. The entire song is thumb strummed with occasional short downward brush strokes of the index finger. Be sure to notice the two long upward thumb strums in the first measure of the last line. Have fun with this happy song!

WEGGI'S SONG

"Greensleeves" is a great song to learn. The holiday tune "What Child Is This?" shares its melody, so we can enjoy it all year long. First, note that it is written in 6/8 time, meaning there are six beats to the measure and every eighth note receives one beat. "Greensleeves" offers new opportunities to increase your skills and expand your repertoire. Notice it is written in the key of G minor. The melody toggles back and forth between major and minor sounds, adding much interest. There are five chords used in the song, so you will get good practice moving your chord hand over the chord-bar buttons.

Even though a short thumb strum is utilized primarily throughout the song, there are a few measures in which a very long thumb strum adds musicality and drama as you accompany the vocal melody. This long thumb strum with a loop in the middle and arrow at its end (starting in measure 9) begins at the bass, and, upon reaching the highest strings, the index finger starts a downward loop. Then, the thumb completes the loop and flows to the highest strings again. Finally, the middle finger or index finger (your choice) strums downward—without a break—back to the bass. These long thumb strums will last for the entire measure.

Twice within the song, there will be long thumb strums that only last three beats, again from the bass to the highest strings, but not returning to the bass. The arrows in the song clearly demonstrate the direction of the strums.

GREENSLEEVES

Chords: Gm, F, Dm, D7, B♭

BEGINNING MELODY PLAYING

Playing melody on the autoharp is a skill that adds much musicality to your performance. Many attempt to learn this skill by trial and error, but if you do not produce a clear and precise melody, the result is not so pleasing. I will show you how to pick melodies that are clear and precise. I know you will enjoy the result!

We must first recognize the individual notes within chords. For example, when the C chord is strummed, you will hear the notes C, E, and G. When the F chord is strummed, you will hear the notes F, A, and C. When the G chord is strummed, you will hear G, B, and D. If the tonic chord is C, then the IV chord will be F and the V chord will be G. So in this case, all notes of the C major scale are heard: C, D, E, F, G, A, and B.

If we are to pick out the melody of a song, rather than simply strum the chords, it helps to know how the individual strings are laid out. Although there are many different autoharps available, my explanation will assume you have a 36-string, 21-chord chromatic Oscar Schmidt autoharp—as this is the most common autoharp. Let's study the layout of the strings so a correct bearing can be determined.

Please observe your autoharp, laying it down in front of you. The locations of the C notes are the 12th, 24th, and 36th strings. In other words, at every third section of the strings, there is another C.

The locations of the G notes are the 7th, 19th, and 31st strings. Please note that the 19th string lies approximately in the center of the autoharp. This is important to know, as the center is easy to distinguish and therefore helps you to locate G and the notes closest to G.

Now, look at the distance between each string—it is only a quarter inch, not much at all. It is important to get a feel for this distance if one is to play accurately. If you are to pick a **half step** from one note to the next (as would be the case between E and F, and B and C), the distance will only be a quarter inch. Take a moment to locate the E and F notes and notice the distance between the two strings. Now, do the same with the B and C strings.

MAJOR SCALES AND MELODY-PICKING PRACTICE

A **whole step** is necessary to move from C to D, D to E, F to G, G to A, and A to B. That whole-step distance is one half inch to three-quarters of an inch. Please take a moment to experiment with playing these two-string combinations.

There are several techniques used to play a melody. One is called **plucking**, and it is designated by the symbol ○. Plucking is accomplished by simply plucking a single string with your index finger.

Another technique is called **pinching**, or **double pinching**. When we pinch a melody—designated by the symbol ⁎—the middle finger picks the melody note as the thumb picks the harmonious string below the melody, a distance of approximately one to three inches. Take a moment and experiment with this technique as you play different melody notes.

As you pinch your melody, be careful to bend only the two knuckles on the middle finger. Never use wrist movement to accomplish the pinch. Also, be careful not to jump the fingers over the strings. In other words, keep the fingers close to the strings—do not lift them up high and then lower them.

The resultant shape of the middle finger to the thumb will be that of an "L," i.e., 90 degrees to each other, as shown in the photo. Keep the thumb and middle finger locked in this position for good control of distance.

Double Pinching L-Shape

The following major scales and melody-picking practice examples allow you to work on what you have just learned. Using these techniques will give you accurate melody and clear sound at all times. Under the notes, I have written the corresponding string numbers (assuming you are playing an Oscar Schmidt autoharp). Notice where the whole steps are in relation to the half steps. Also, please observe the fingering in the tablature, as I change it after the first two lines to give you more practice.

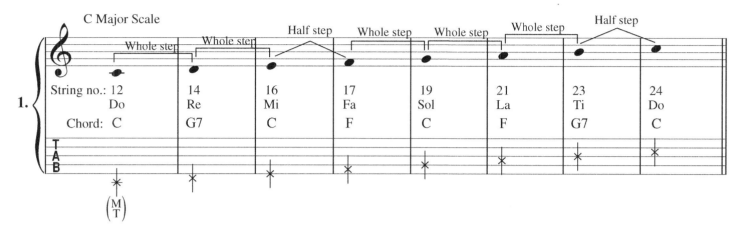

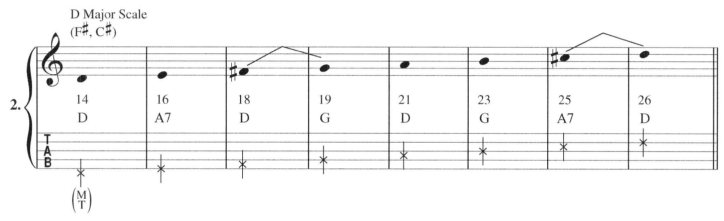

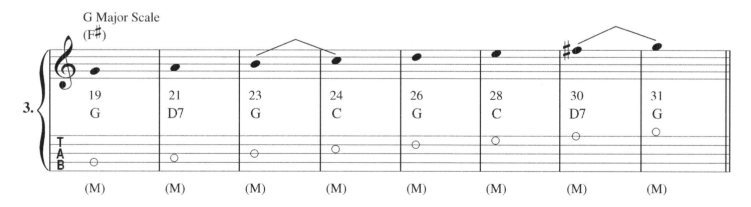

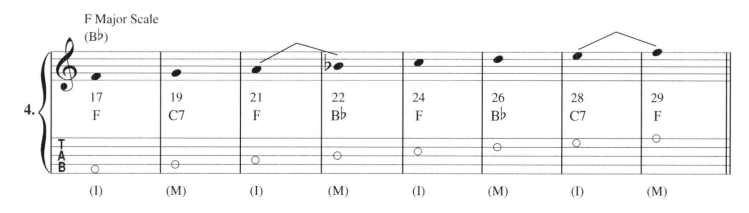

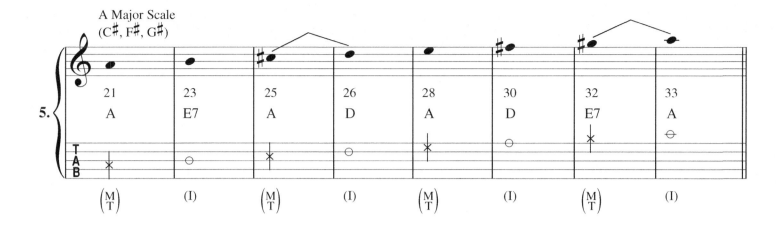

MELODY AIDS

The templates on page 71 are designed to assist you in plucking or pinching the correct strings. This template was made specifically for an Oscar Schmidt 21-chord, 36-string autoharp, but it may be customized to fit other autoharps, as well. With permission from Oscar Schmidt, I have included these for your use.

Cut out one of the templates and place it directly under the lowest string. Adhere it with clear tape. As you can see, C is typically located on the 3rd, 12th, 24th, and 36th strings. G is typically the 19th string. If these string locations match what is on your own harp, this template is ready for you to use. The top template does not reflect string names; you may customize this template for your own autoharp, writing in middle G and all the Cs.

Place melody aid under correct strings
and hold with clear tape.

MELODY-PICKING PRACTICE NO. 1 (PINCHING)

Let's continue working on our pinching technique using the same scales as on page 41. Remember to always keep your middle finger and thumb at a 90-degree angle to each other and hold them in this position. Keeping these fingers relatively rigid allows you to control the angle and thereby pinch the correct strings. In addition, as you pinch the melody note with your middle finger, pinch the harmony with the thumb more softly. It is the top note that is to be heard more strongly, not the lower note.

Another tab symbol I like to use is ⌢ , and it signifies **sustain**. This symbol is on the tab staff.

Now, we're ready to begin pinching the C major scale (see examples that follow). Begin on the strings numbered as shown between the two staves in each example; in this example, start on string 12, middle C. Then, move about a half inch upward to string 14, D, then to string 16, E, and then only a half step (quarter inch) to string 17, F. Progress in this way, making certain you are on the correct strings as indicated in the music. Remember, in major scales, the two half steps appear between notes 3 and 4, and again between 7 and 8. This pattern is a good guide for you to remember, as it will help you move your pinch the correct distance each time. At the same time as you are pinching the scale, your chord hand will be playing the necessary chords for the key of C: C, G7, and F.

Our second scale takes us to the key of D, and your chord hand will be playing D, A7, and G. Again, begin on the string as numbered and proceed as before. The only difference is that for this scale, I would like you to pinch on beat 1, and then strum on beats 2, 3, and 4. There will be no sustaining or holding of the notes. Remember to only move a quarter inch between notes 3 and 4, and 7 and 8.

The third scale is in the key of F, so your chord hand will be playing F, C7, and B♭. The fourth scale is in the key of G, so the chord hand will play G, D7, and C. The fifth scale is in the key of A, and the chord hand will play A, E7, and D.

Please note the consistency of the half steps in each of these scales. Always remember this pattern: whole step, whole step, half step, whole step, whole step, whole step, half step. For the fingers on your strumming hand, this translates to: half inch, half inch, quarter inch, half inch, half inch, half inch, quarter inch.

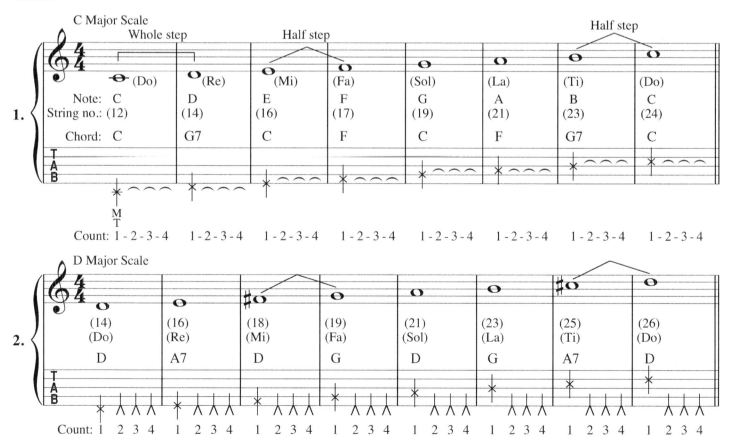

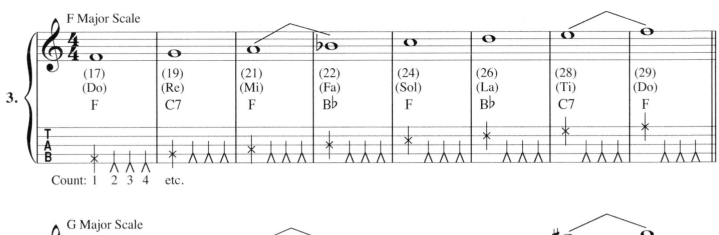

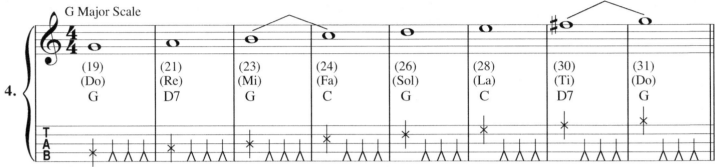

MELODY-PICKING PRACTICE NO. 2 (PINCHING)

It is important to develop the flexibility of not only pinching the correct strings as you play the scales, but also playing notes of different values in consecutive measures. In Practice No. 1, all the measures within one scale have had notes of the same value; now, the notes will be of differing values. In Practice No. 2, notice the sustain marks on the tab clef. Remember, these show you the beats to be held until the next note is played. Take your time to count the beats as shown, as you pinch the correct notes of the scale with the middle finger and thumb in the controlled shape of an "L."

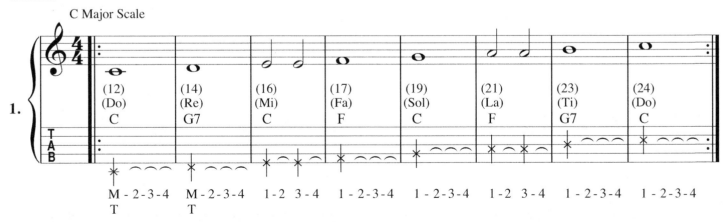

2.

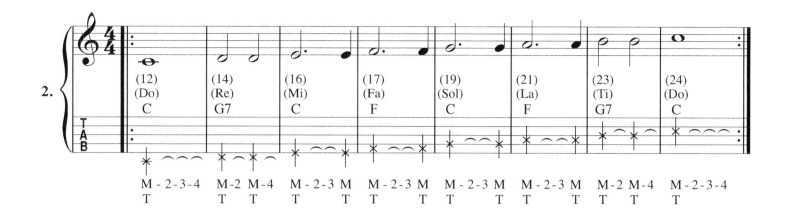

3.

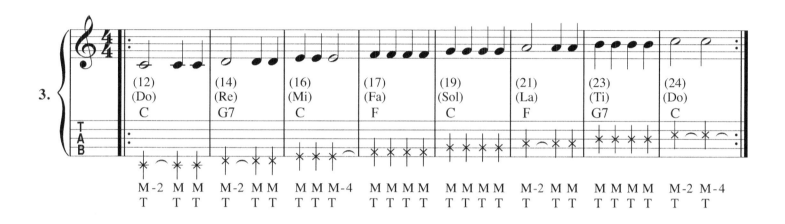

4.

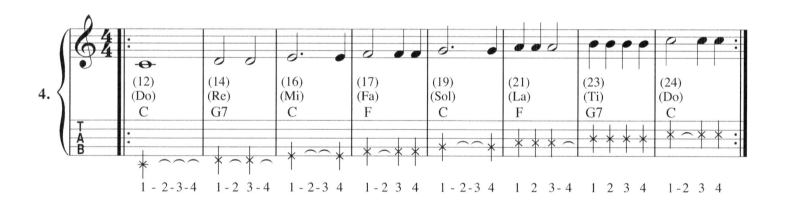

5.

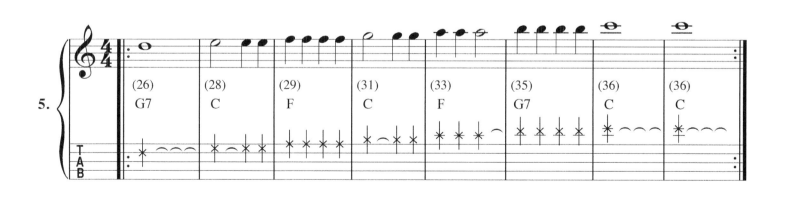

"Wildwood Flower" is one of the most popular autoharp folk songs, so let's add it to your repertoire. It is a great song for practicing pinches and short thumb strums, especially when combined with the short back brush of the index finger.

WILDWOOD FLOWER

Chords: C, F, G7, C7

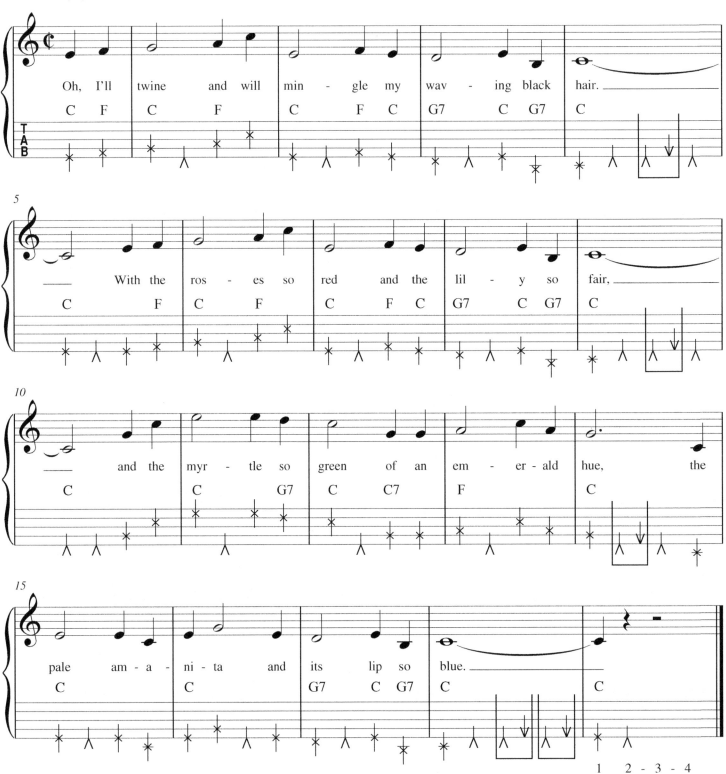

MELODY-PICKING PRACTICE NO. 3 (PINCHING AND PLUCKING)

Now that you have learned the pinch technique, you will find much value in adding the plucking technique to your bag of skills. Remember, a pluck is designated by a ○ sign. It is played on one string only, typically the melody itself, by plucking with your index finger. Although this seems very easy, it requires good focus and practice to develop the necessary accuracy.

In Practice No. 3, we will be using the C major scale on all four examples, all of which begin on string 12. The first two examples are in 4/4 time, and the next two are in 3/4 time.

These exercises will help you develop the flexibility to move from a pinch to a pluck, from a short thumb strum to a pluck, from a short thumb strum to a pinch, and to any combination that may be presented to you. In other words, this exercise encompasses all you have learned so far. Once you understand and can easily play Practice No. 3, with its various rhythms, you can play almost any song presented to you.

As a reminder, please review the tab staves below before you begin playing the exercises. (Remember, they illustrate the various thumb and finger combinations you have learned, and the bracket around each combination represents the actions occurring within one beat.)

MELODY-PICKING PRACTICE NO. 4 (SYNCOPATED RHYTHMS)

In this section, you will be learning to play a syncopated rhythm, step by step. All the examples are in 2/4 time. Starting with the first example, notice that all the notes are eighth notes. Remember that each eighth note receives half a beat. Eighth notes are counted "one and, two and," etc. Every action within a bracket receives one full count, "one and." Begin with a pinch and follow with a pluck as you count "one and."

The second example introduces sixteenth notes, each receiving a quarter beat. Four sixteenth notes are counted "one-e-and-uh" or "two-e-and-uh," and so on, depending on which beat they fall. In measure 3, you would count "one and, two and-uh," as the sixteenth notes are pinched and plucked on the "and-uh." In measure 4, the sixteenth notes replace an eighth note on the count of "2." This measure would be counted out as "one and, two-e-and," as the sixteenth notes are pinched and plucked on the "two-e" count. In measure 7, there are four sixteenth notes all occurring within one beat. This measure would be counted "one and, two-e-and-uh." I have inserted a sustain within the brackets to remind you to hold the eighth note twice as long as the sixteenth note.

The third example is similar to the second example. A tip that will help you practice these examples is to count each measure aloud prior to picking up your autoharp. In addition, it may help you to make the pinch and pluck motions with your hand as you count. Do this several times until you are comfortable counting correctly, and then pick up your autoharp and practice the examples.

The fourth example features syncopation, which is produced when a dotted note is followed by a note that is one quarter the count of the first note. In the first measure, the first two notes are counted "one-e-and-uh," with the dotted eighth note receiving the count of "one-e-and" and the sixteenth note receiving the count of "uh." This count is typically shortened to include only the rhythms that are played: "one-uh, two-uh," etc. Notice the sustain marks indicating when the pinch and pluck will occur. This pattern is repeated until the last measure.

The last example has the same syncopated rhythm as the fourth one, however, within each bracketed count, your chord hand will alternate between two chord bars: C and G7, C and F, G7 and F, and so forth. The purpose is to increase your chord hand's dexterity as you move up and down the strings with your strumming hand. This is such an important skill to develop, especially as you learn to play fast songs from many genres. You are now an accomplished player of the autoharp and are fully prepared to move to the intermediate level where melody picking is enjoyed so much!

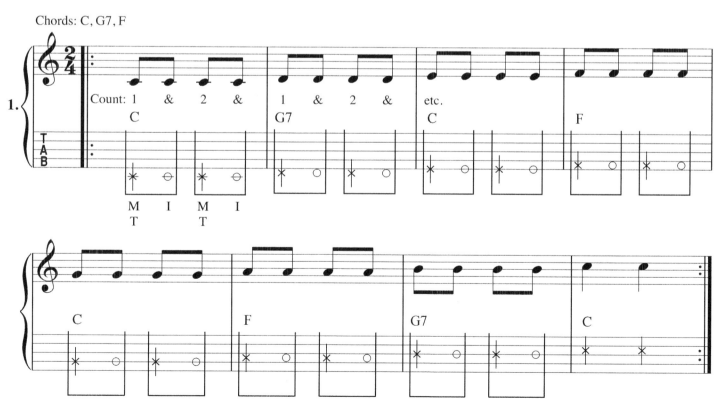

2.

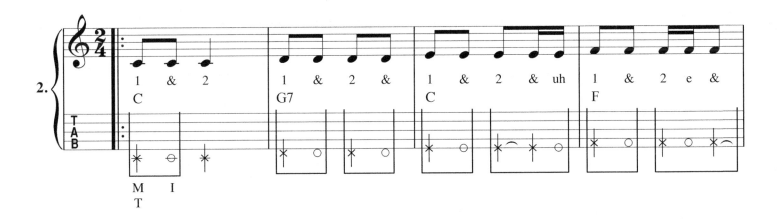

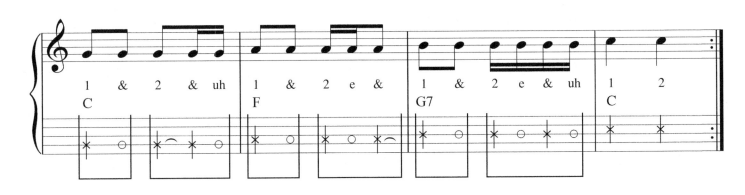

3.

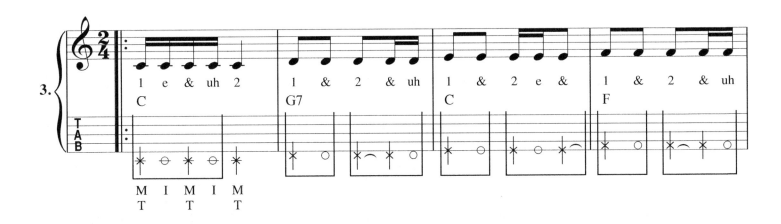

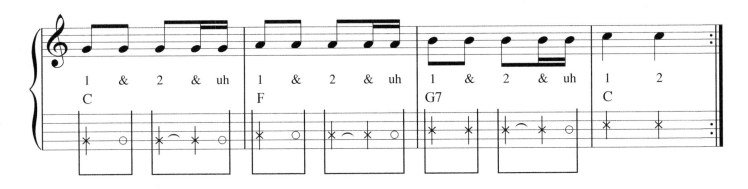

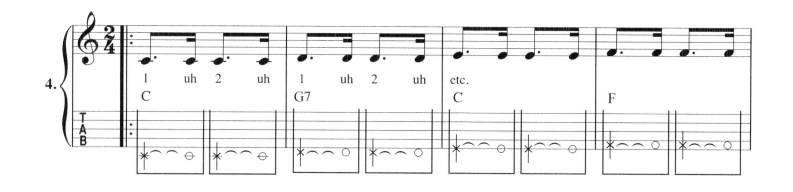

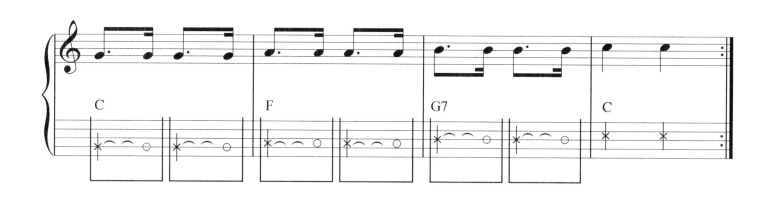

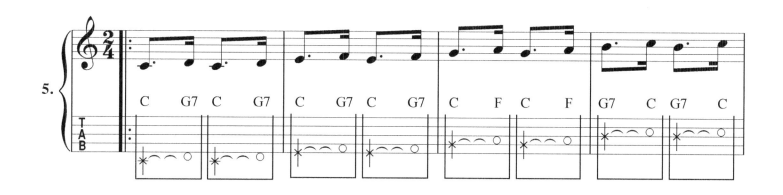

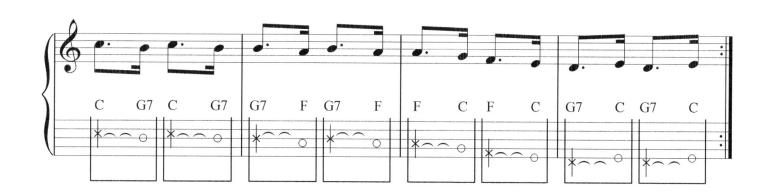

MORE STRUMMING TECHNIQUES

Before moving on to more songs with melody picking, let's build on our strumming technique with a few more examples.

As with the previous sections, I'll explain each of the examples on the next page, and then you can practice them individually or together as one big exercise.

Our first example shows a long thumb strum with the strumming hand. Starting at the bass end of the strings, strum upward toward the high strings. Each measure asks for a different long thumb strum: first a quarter note for one beat, then a half note for two beats, a dotted half note for three beats, and finally a whole note for four beats.

The second example is similar to the first as far as note values, but the strum is a long downward strum with the middle finger, starting at the high strings and dragging downward to the bass strings.

The third example features the same note values as the preceding two examples. The swirling lines and loops are how I demonstrate an **arpeggio strum**. In this example, each arpeggio strum becomes more technical as the note is held longer. The quarter-note arpeggio begins at the bottom of the bass strings with the thumb strumming upward to the high strings. At the apex, or top of the swirl, the middle finger takes the place of the thumb by returning back to the bass strings. This is a flowing motion with no break, as the middle finger picks up where the thumb leaves off.

Measure 2 of the third example illustrates a **single-looping arpeggio strum**. This half-note arpeggio strum begins on the bass strings with the thumb moving upward to the high strings, at which time the index finger takes over and strums downward a short distance as it begins a small loop. At the bottom of the small loop, the thumb resumes the strum back up to the high strings. Finally, the middle finger strums all the way down to the bass strings.

Measure 3 of the third example shows a **double-looping arpeggio strum**. This dotted half note is long enough to allow for two loops, hence, a double-looping arpeggio strum. As before, the thumb begins the upward motion from the bass strings to the high strings, at which time the index finger takes over and strums downward a short distance as it begins a small loop. At the bottom of the small loop, the thumb resumes the strum back up to the high strings again. The middle finger begins the second loop downward as it makes the second small loop. The thumb again picks up the upward strumming movement of the strings. At the top of the strings, the middle finger will now strum all the way down to the bass strings again.

Measure 4 of the third example shows a **triple-looping arpeggio strum**. This whole note is held for four beats and is now long enough to allow for three loops. The technique is identical to that of the double-looping arpeggio strum, only adding one more loop.

The key to success with these arpeggios is to take your time and practice for evenness, without breaking the flow of the strumming on the strings. The effect is very lovely and dramatic, and it is often used when playing slow classical music, hymns, and other slow songs. Enjoy your new technique!

Use D chord throughout

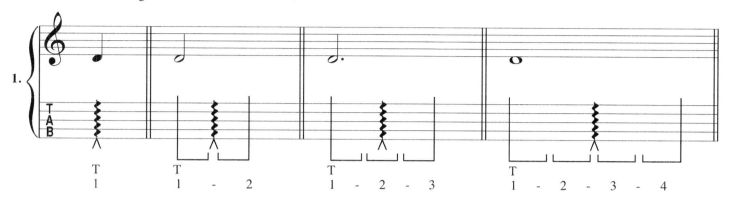

1.

T	T		T			T			
1	1	-	2	1	-	2	-	3	
			1	-	2	-	3	-	4

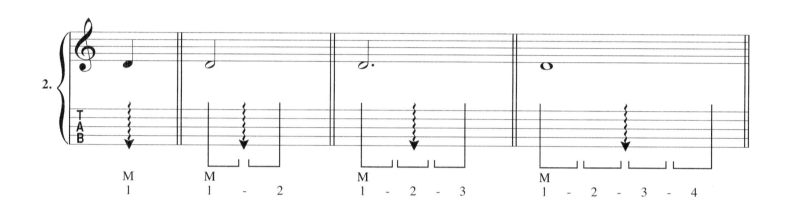

2.

M	M		M			M			
1	1	-	2	1	-	2	-	3	
			1	-	2	-	3	-	4

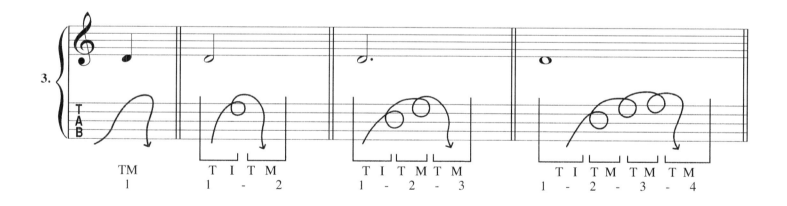

3.

TM	T I T M	T I T M T M	T I T M T M T M
1	1 - 2	1 - 2 - 3	1 - 2 - 3 - 4

MELODY-PICKING SONGS

Now, let's put our strumming and melody playing to use with some great songs.

"Will the Circle Be Unbroken" is written in cut time. Remember, cut time is actually 2/2 time, so there are two beats per measure and each half note receives one beat. Also, in cut time, a quarter note receives only one half beat. For this song, it will be easiest to count "one and, two and" for each measure. For the first (pickup) measure, come in on "two and."

Take a close look at all the ties. If two half notes are tied, you will hold the note for two counts (1 + 1). If a whole note and a half note are tied, you will hold the note for three counts (2 + 1). See if you can identify these tied notes and determine which are held for two counts and which are held for three counts.

This song sounds best at a moderate tempo, so start slowly to get the correct rhythm along with the strum pattern. Gradually work your way up to a moderate tempo.

 WILL THE CIRCLE BE UNBROKEN

Chords: G, C, D7

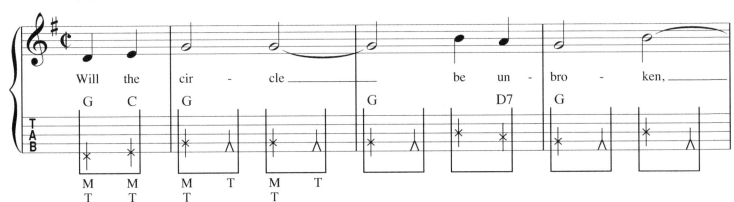

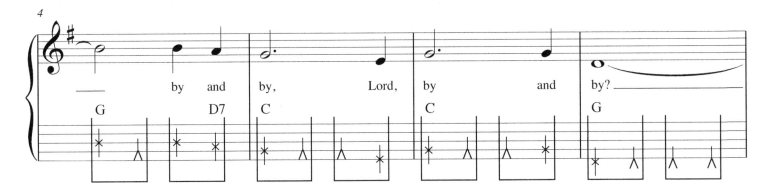

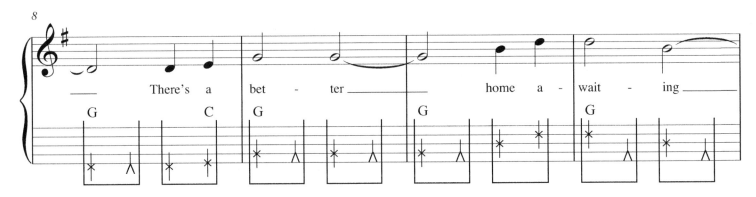

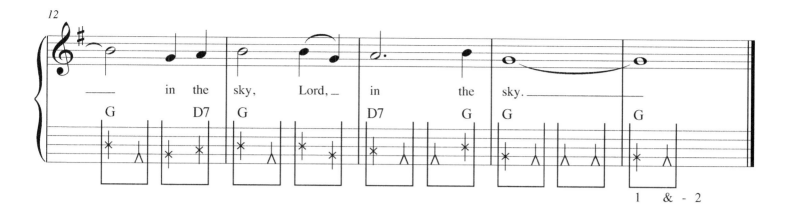

The next tune features pinching and plucking. Practice slowly at first to make sure you get these techniques right.

HUSH, LITTLE BABY

Chords: G, C, D7

"The Four Marys" is a lovely traditional Scottish song played in a slow waltz rhythm. Please notice the long **thumb runs** that end in a pinch in the first and third lines ⁕.

The thumb run involves an upward thumb strum along with a pinch as the strum approaches the melody strings. The strum continues upward until about three quarters of an inch to one inch before the melody strings, at which time the pinch finishes off the technique.

THE FOUR MARYS

Chords: C, G7, F, Am, Dm

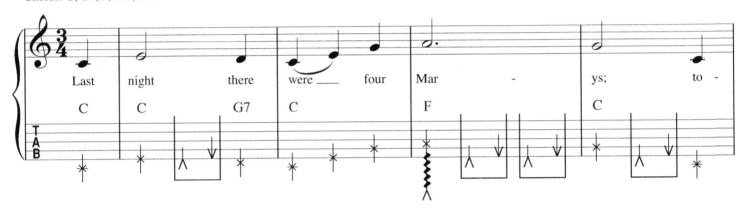

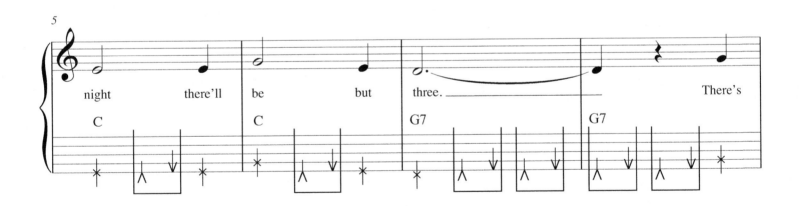

Our next song, "Old Joe Clark (No. 2)," is a rather simple song, but we are going to add a **modulation** to it. Modulation is the changing of one key to another within the same song. The first half of the song is written in G, then at measure 15, it modulates quickly to the key of A. Modulating always adds a lot of musicality and interest to a song. To modulate in this particular song, simply move your middle finger from G up to A. The progression over the chord bars in the key of A, throughout the second half of the song, mimics the same progression that was played in the key of G.

The song is written in an **A-B format**, which means there are two distinct sections of the song. In some A-B songs, there is a verse followed by a chorus. Because this song is transposed after the first A and B parts, and repeats those parts but in a different key, there are two A and B parts, i.e., A-B + A-B.

There are several other interesting aspects to this song: one is that it is written in all majors (the I, IV, and ♭VII chords), which makes the song easy to play.

There are also many repeats. When you finish the eighth measure, return to the beginning of the song. Then play through it again. This completes the A part of the song.

As you begin the B part, you will play to the next repeat: the first ending (indicated by a bracket and the number "1"). When you finish the first ending, return to the beginning of part B and play through measures 9 and 10 again. Then, skip the first ending and proceed to the second ending (indicated by a bracket and the number "2").

Now, you are ready to play the second set of A and B parts, in the key of A. The repeats function similarly to the first half of the song, but this time with two sets of first and second endings. I have purposefully left out the lyrics so you can concentrate on playing this tricky song form.

Chords: G, C, F, A, D
Keys: G → A

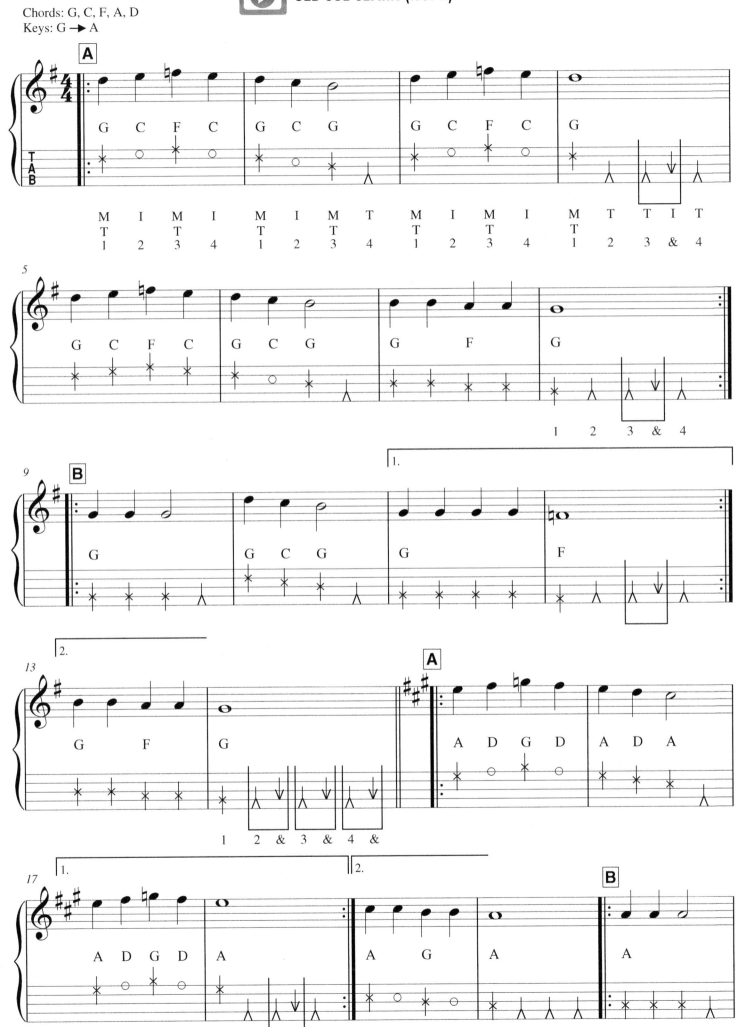

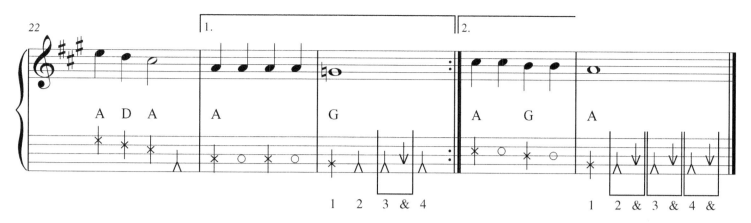

"Water Is Wide" is a traditional song played by many musicians. We'll play it in the key of F major. Written in 4/4 time, the counting is very straightforward. Notice, however, that every whole note is tied to a quarter note for a total of five beats (4 beats for the whole note + 1 beat for the quarter note).

▶ **WATER IS WIDE**

Chords: F, C7, B♭, Dm, Gm, Am

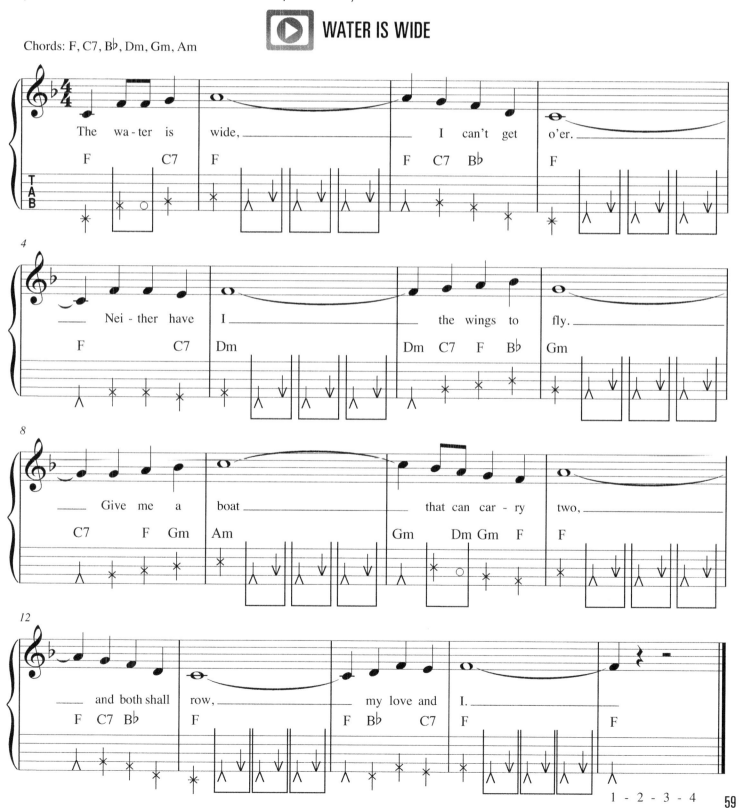

59

Following is another traditional tune in the key of F major.

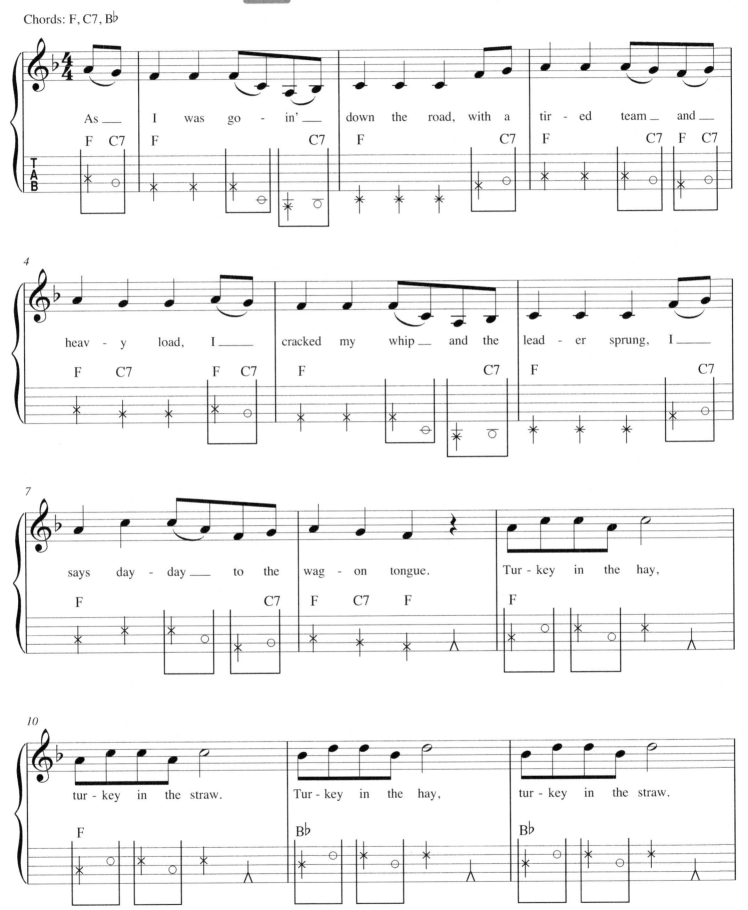

TURKEY IN THE STRAW

Chords: F, C7, B♭

"Amazing Grace (No. 2)" on the next page has a few strumming techniques that were not used in the first version of the tune. Unlike the first version, which featured a modulation (key change), this arrangement remains in the key of G throughout. This version also contains a thumb run.

There are two measures that contain syncopated notes: measure 9 and measure 11. Practice clapping out these two measures until you are comfortable with the rhythms. Then, practice the strumming in these measures until you are comfortable with the patterns that accompany the melody notes.

Please note that there is a single-loop arpeggio in measure 7, followed by a simple long thumb strum in the next measure. Refer back to page 52 to review how to execute this technique.

It is a wise and efficient practice to isolate the more technical measures of a song and work on these alone before attempting to play the entire song. In this way, you will be able to maintain a constant, although slower, rhythm, which in time will increase to a more favorable speed.

AMAZING GRACE (NO. 2)

Chords: G, D7, C

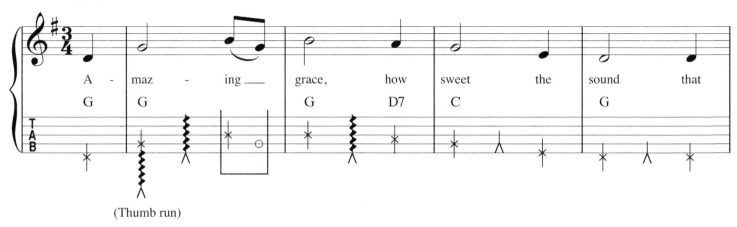

(Thumb run)

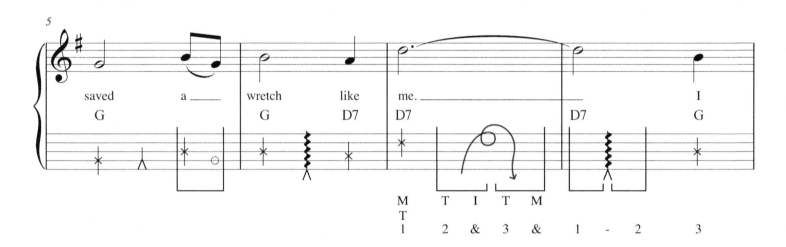

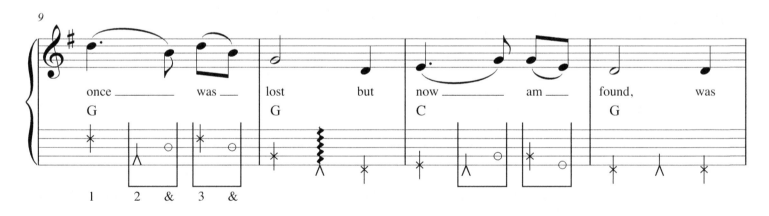

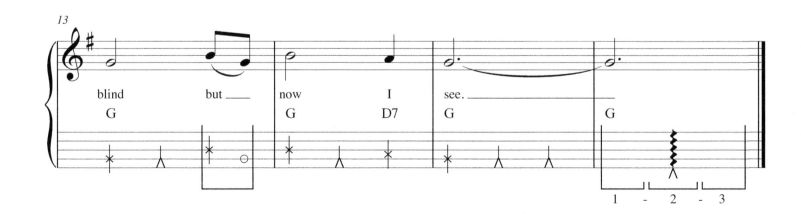

"Lullaby" is a familiar old tune written in the key of C in 3/4 time. The pickup notes are on the third count, so you would begin playing on "three and."

The only syncopation occurs in the first and third full measures. In each occurrence, there is a short upward thumb strum followed by a pluck on the count of "and." Take your time and let the melody flow smoothly as you enjoy this relaxing, sweet song.

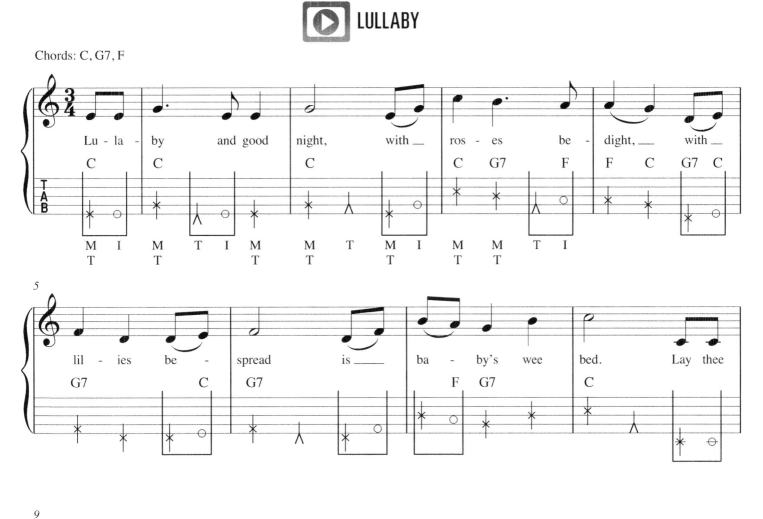

LULLABY

Chords: C, G7, F

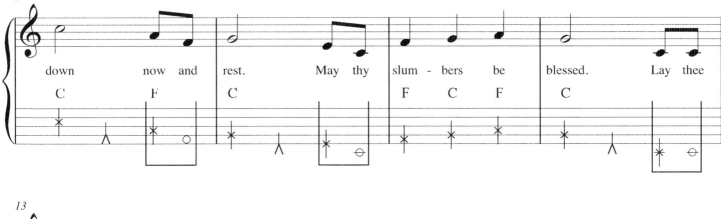

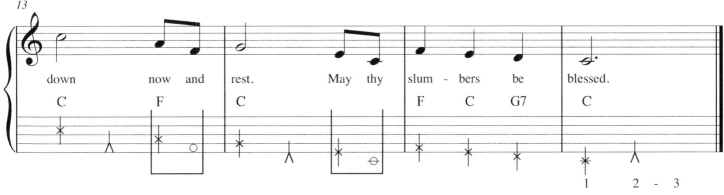

"Scarborough Fair" is in A minor and in 3/4 time. It changes to a major sound in the third line and returns to its minor tonality in the fourth line, ultimately adding beauty to this traditional song.

Please review the tablature, which features pinches, short thumb strums, plucks, and then a long downward strum with the middle finger in measures 5 and 15. The only syncopation is in measures 2 and 3. Once you are familiar with the strumming patterns, play the song through slowly, maintaining the waltz rhythm in an even flow.

SCARBOROUGH FAIR

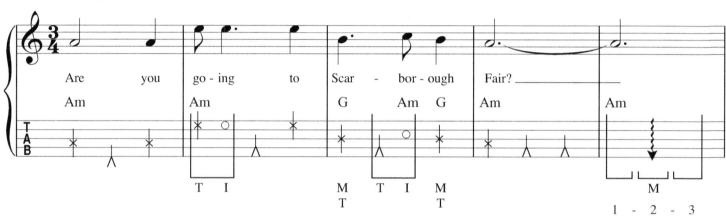

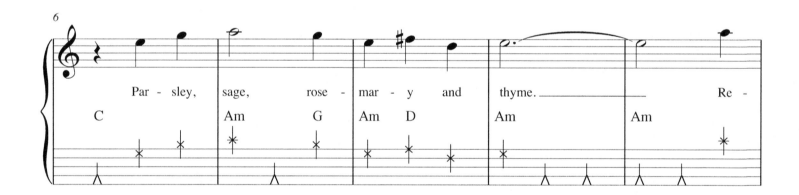

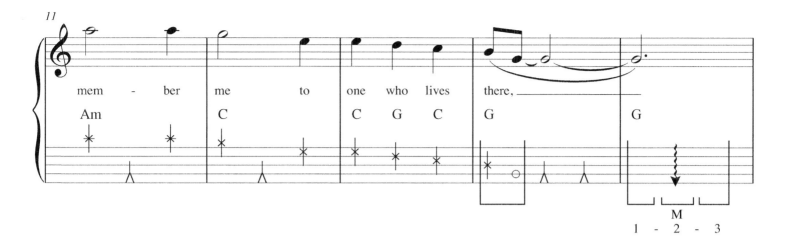

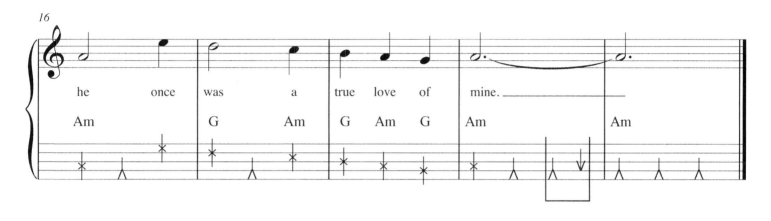

The next song, "Wayfaring Stranger," is in the key of D minor and in 3/4 time. It is a good song for practicing pinches and a variety of strums. Please notice there are many long thumb strums, as well as an occasional short thumb strum. The long thumb strums are held for a full count in this song. Also, there is a frequently repeated strum pattern that starts with a pinch and is quickly followed by a long thumb strum, as in the first full measure. To play this pattern, pinch on the count of "one," then immediately begin the long thumb strum on counts "and – two." Next, pinch on each of the following notes as you count "and – three – and." Again, it will help if you form the finger motions in the air prior to placing them on the autoharp, counting out loud as you proceed.

Notice the fermata at the end of the song. Remember, this tells you to hold the note longer, in this case, longer than three beats. You will often see the fermata at the end of a slow song.

To help you get started, the string numbers for the first line are shown below the notes.

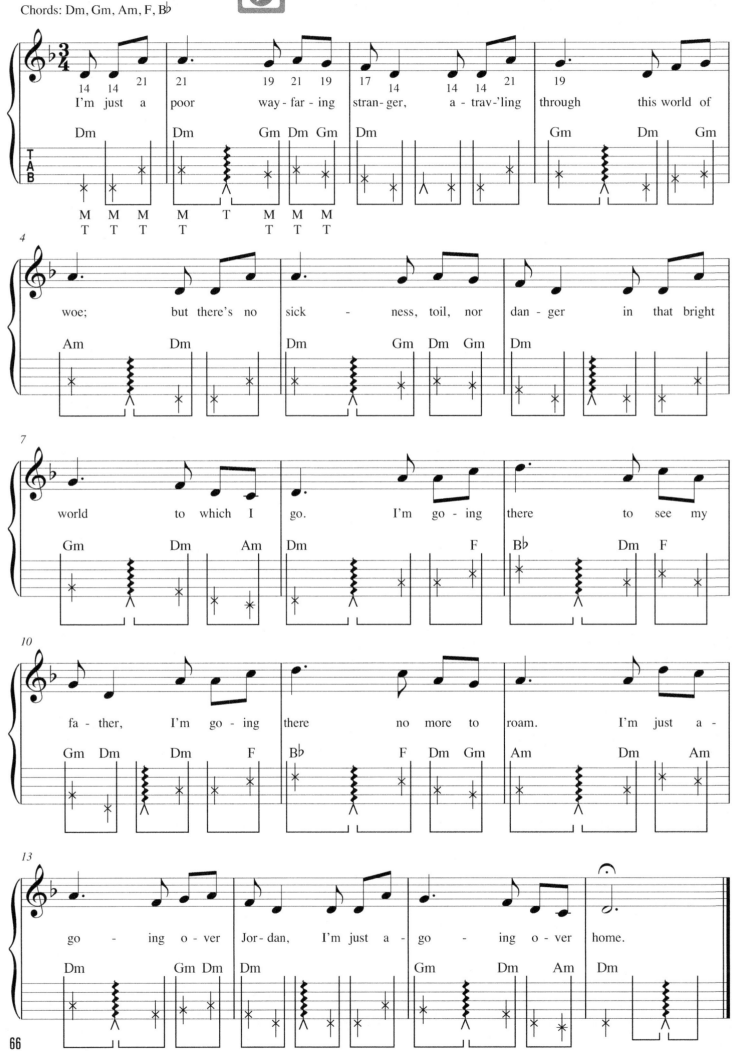

"16ths Melody" is in the key of F, and it is in 2/4 time. Please notice the sustain in almost every bracket, indicating that the preceding pinch is to be held—in this case, for the duration of an additional sixteenth note. Each measure is counted as "one-e-and-uh, two-e-and-uh." Within the first bracket, the pinch is made on the count of "one," sustain, then pinch on "and" and pluck on "uh." It often helps to clap the rhythm as you proceed through the measures, prior to playing them on the autoharp. Follow that exercise with the correct hand motions and then play the melody on the autoharp.

▶ 16THS MELODY

"The Cuckoo" is a cute song with lyrics that include yodeling. Written in 3/4 time in the key of F, it utilizes pinches, plucks, short thumb strums, and syncopated rhythms. Note that measure 9 has three fermatas—here, you will play three thumb runs. This completes the A part of the song.

The B part of the song is a bit different, as it is the yodeling section. It is syncopated, so you may find it helpful to clap out the rhythms and then make the appropriate pinching, plucking, and strumming motions with your hand prior to picking up your autoharp. This truly demystifies and simplifies learning each song.

 THE CUCKOO

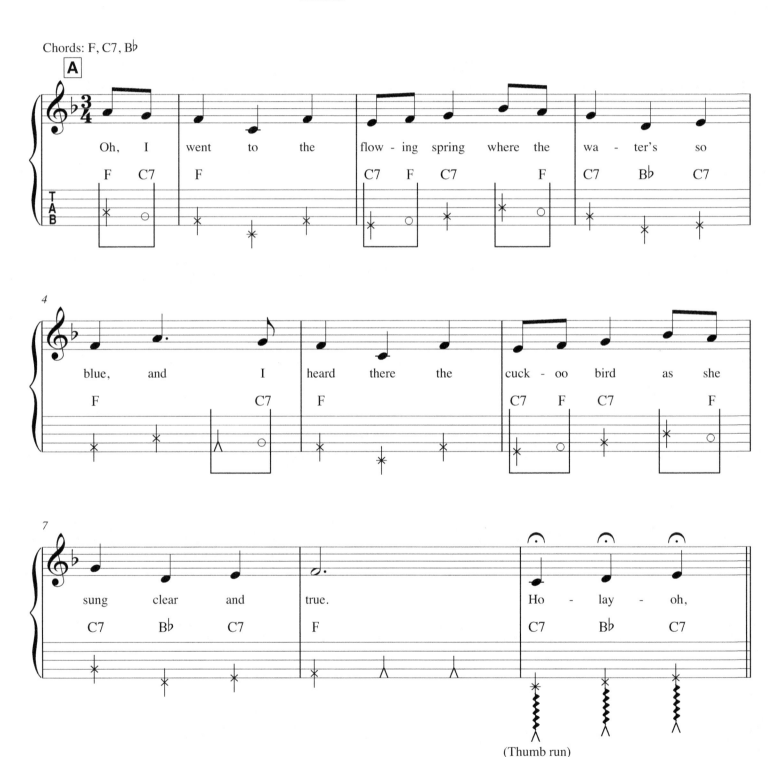

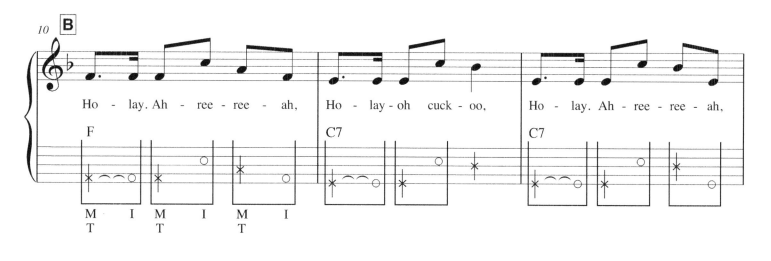

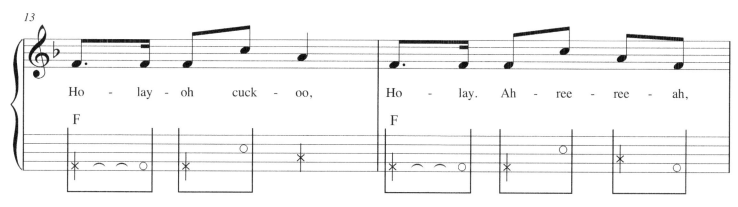

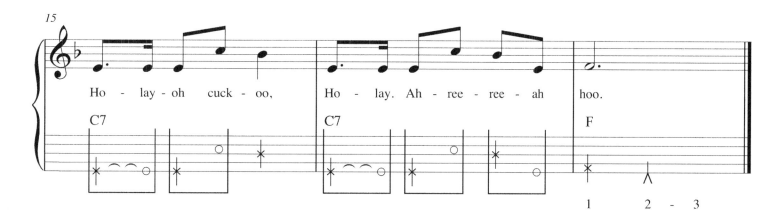

Our final song, "The Blacksmith," is a two-chord song, so your chord hand will not be so busy. However, your strumming hand will be quite active playing the syncopated rhythm. The rhythm pattern inside the brackets is repeated many times. Once you are comfortable with this pattern, you can easily play the song.

Let's study the pattern within the brackets, remembering that all action within a bracket takes place in one beat. The pattern begins with a pinch on the dotted eighth note, which is sustained for the duration of three sixteenth notes, and is followed by a sixteenth note. It is counted as "two-e-and-a" or "four-e-and-a," as the case may be. The pinch is held for a total of three sixteenth notes, while the pluck is held for only one sixteenth note.

With the exception of the final measure, every measure has this pattern as its fourth beat. Now, practice this pattern on its own by first clapping and counting. Then, let your strumming hand pinch and pluck the pattern on the autoharp, over and over until you are completely comfortable with it. You are now ready to play the song with the addition of the other pinches and strums. If you are playing it rhythmically, you can actually hear the pounding of the blacksmith's hammer on his anvil.

THE BLACKSMITH

Chords: C, G7

Oh, the black - smith's a fine stur - dy fel - low, hard his

C   C   G7

M   I   M   M   I   M   M   I

T   T   T   T   T

hands but his heart's true and mel - low; see him stand there, his huge bel - lows

G7   C   C

blow - ing   with his strong, brawn - y arms free and bare;   see the

C   C   G7   C

fire in the fur - nace a - glow - ing   bright, its

C   C

spar - kle, its flash and its glare.

C   G7   C

1   2   3 - 4

70

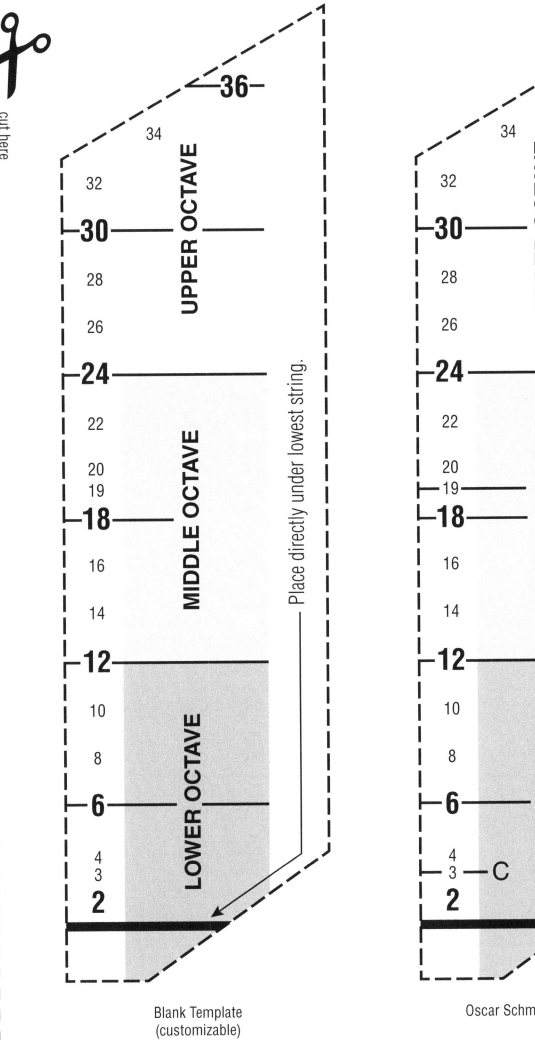

cut here

Blank Template
(customizable)

Oscar Schmidt-Type Template